*Culinary Arts Institute*®

# COOKING FRENCH
## THE NEW WAY

*Featured in cover photo:*
Steamed Red Snapper Oriental, 51

# COOKING FRENCH THE NEW WAY

Sue Spitler and
The Culinary Arts Institute staff
Edward Finnegan: Executive Editor

Book designed and coordinated by Charles Bozett
Illustrations by Seymour Fleishman
Cover photo: Bob Scott Studios   Inside photos: Zdenek Piveka

Adventures in Cooking SERIES

# COOKING FRENCH
## THE NEW WAY

ÉPICERIE

POISSONNERIE

*Culinary Arts Institute*®
A DIVISION OF DELAIR/CONSOLIDATED   new york

Copyright © 1980 by
Delair Publishing Company, Inc.
420 Lexington Avenue,
New York, New York 10017

Library of Congress Catalogue Card Number: 80-65527
ISBN: 0-8326-0609-X

# CONTENTS

# THE NEW FRENCH REVOLUTION

It was bound to happen. Like a pendulum, most things carried to extremes will swing back, rebounding often to something completely new, or at least to a more normal state.

This is precisely what has been happening in the last few years to French cooking. The old *grand cuisine* of France, acclaimed as the world's best and most highly refined of all time, is losing its position of unquestioned supremacy.

In its place one finds the young and tender sproutings of a very new way of cooking in France, so new that a name for it has not yet been generally agreed upon. It goes by such designations as *la nouvelle cuisine, cuisine minceur, cuisine diététique,* the *new low-high cuisine,* and even *la nouvelle revolution française.* In this book we will simply call it the New French Cooking.

Indeed, it is a new revolution in France, one all the more remarkable because it is taking place right within the ranks of the great chefs of France, among those culinary artists who spent years of their lives learning the disciplines and honing their skills to become the best practitioners of the grand, classic cuisine. The number of these revolutionaries may still be small, but it continues to grow. And, most significantly, they include some of France's most famous chefs as well as many French chefs practicing their trade in the United States and other countries.

Very simply, these chefs are rebelling against the old classic cuisine because they find it irrelevant today. In an era when high-fat diets are known to be hazardous to health and most people want to keep their weight near normal, a style of cooking which emphasizes lavish amounts of butter, eggs, cream, heavy sauces, and rich pastry is out of place.

The classic cuisine is also rigid and does not allow chefs to vary procedures and invent new dishes. It has remained static for nearly a century, since the reign of Escoffier, the grand master.

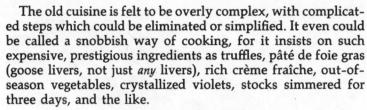

The old cuisine is felt to be overly complex, with complicated steps which could be eliminated or simplified. It even could be called a snobbish way of cooking, for it insists on such expensive, prestigious ingredients as truffles, pâté de foie gras (goose livers, not just *any* livers), rich crème fraîche, out-of-season vegetables, crystallized violets, stocks simmered for three days, and the like.

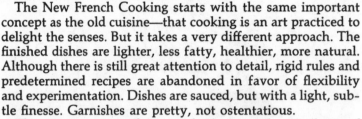

## A LIGHT, NATURAL CUISINE

The New French Cooking starts with the same important concept as the old cuisine—that cooking is an art practiced to delight the senses. But it takes a very different approach. The finished dishes are lighter, less fatty, healthier, more natural. Although there is still great attention to detail, rigid rules and predetermined recipes are abandoned in favor of flexibility and experimentation. Dishes are sauced, but with a light, subtle finesse. Garnishes are pretty, not ostentatious.

There is a great emphasis on freshness and naturalness of ingredients. If a vegetable in a particular dish is out of season, the New French chefs feel it is better to substitute one that is available fresh, rather than use a canned or frozen vegetable. Vegetables are not heavily sauced or buttered, so that the natural flavor and texture can dominate. In the classic cuisine it sometimes does not matter if vegetables are frozen or canned because rich hollandaise and cream sauces often adorn them, masking and altering the basic flavor. Instead, in the New French Cooking one can enjoy the vegetable in its own right. Cooking also stops while there is just a touch of crispness left.

The use of cream, butter, fats, flour, and eggs is cut to an absolute minimum. Sometimes a vegetable purée becomes the thickener of a sauce. Or just a little arrowroot or cornstarch is added to give body, but not to create a really thick sauce. Reduction of cooking liquid also can give a slight thickness. Some creamy sauces are made, but they may use a blend of low-fat cheeses (cottage, pot, ricotta) and yogurt.

The new cuisine also borrows liberally from the heritage of French country cooking, considered much too "low" or peasantlike for classic cuisine adherents. It also borrows from foreign countries, particularly the Orient. Outside influences are at work in France, as well as in most countries of the world in this modern age. In cooking, the New French chefs borrow ideas, then refine them and adapt them to yield a distinctive, still quite French result.

## AN END TO THE GRAND SAUCES

But what about the béarnaise, Bordelaise, béchamel, velouté, espagnole, Bercy, Mornay, and all the other classic sauces which form the backbone of the grand cuisine of France? Most have virtually been tossed out the window, which is perhaps the most compelling reason why the new style of cooking has been hailed as revolutionary.

One problem is that sauces (and also stuffings) often become more important than the basic food they adorn. At times one can't even taste the meat beneath, as with that classic triumph, Saddle of Veal Orloff.

Another problem is that the mastery of a set repertoire of

many dozens, even hundreds, of sauces and their precise method of preparation is essential for all classic French chefs. Yet this is where the absurdity of the old cuisine becomes most apparent. Most sauces begin with a basic stock which must simmer long hours. Then the sauce itself must be cooked and stirred. On top of that there are several families of sauces which begin with one mother sauce, then add another whole set of ingredients for the variation. To pile insult on injury, the tasty pan juices which cook out of roasts and steaks often are not even used; a separately prepared sauce is poured on top.

In the New French Cooking, sauces not only have been lightened of their richness, they have been liberated. Stocks, if used at all, are simple and don't require long cooking for reduction. In creating sauces, the chef or home cook is free to experiment and is not bound to a set of rules one hundred years old. Many dishes use the juice of the particular meat, poultry, or fish being cooked to create a sauce. It's almost a case of "anything goes" as long as the end result is a sauce that is light, delectable, and subtle—allowing the basic food being sauced to take center stage.

### A HEALTHIER STYLE

The New French Cooking fits much better into today's life-styles, since people in Europe and America want to eat less, eat lighter, and have foods that are more natural. People are concerned about becoming overweight and about dietary fats and cholesterol. To maintain a thin body on the old cuisine was a matter of feast and famine—gorging on elegant, rich, seven-course meals followed by periods of starvation. The new cuisine allows one to eat sensibly and enjoyably every day.

After cooking for a while in this new manner, it soon becomes a way of life. Other foods probably will taste overly rich to you and may sit like a heavy lump in your stomach.

The new way of cooking and eating should not be considered a reducing diet, although some chefs have designed recipes and menus low enough in calories to qualify for a weight-losing regime. Rather, it could be looked at as a way to eat very well every day in the gourmet French manner and still maintain your present weight.

### NOT ALL IS NEW

Even though the pendulum has swung quite far in the opposite direction, not everything has changed in French cooking. And of course, many French chefs still insist that the grand classic cuisine should remain intact.

In both the old and the new styles, fine cooking is considered as an important and admirable skill. Chefs still pay great attention to detail and take extreme pride in their craftsmanship. Food is an art form with both the old and the new. Arrangements of platters and garnishes are always beautifully done. The difference is a matter of degree; the grand cuisine often is ostentatious and snobbish in its embellishments.

Basic cookery methods remain the same: roasting, broiling, braising, stewing, poaching, beating and folding egg whites, thickenings, cooking times, and so on. You do not have to

learn a new set of cookery techniques, although some applications will be different. Some old procedures may no longer be used, such as frying and preliminary browning of meat in fat.

Sautéeing onions in butter has also been abandoned. It was a time-honored tradition of many old-cuisine recipes, as well as recipes from America and many other countries. New French Cooking proponents say this repetitive sautéeing is not necessary and only adds extra calories. To get rid of the volatile and undesirably sharp flavors (the reason why sautéeing of onions is done in the first place), they can be simmered in a little stock or wine, uncovered.

In designing this book, the CULINARY ARTS INSTITUTE has kept in mind the American kitchen and American ingredients. The recipes were tested by professional home economists using standard American appliances and utensils. There are certain French-style utensils—certain pans and molds, a food processor, garlic press, fish poacher, etc.—that are nice to have. See pages 11–14 for suggestions of items for stocking your kitchen in the French manner, but most of the recipes in this book can be prepared with equipment in an average American kitchen.

The recipes are also designed with ingredients available in food stores in this country. For some recipes you may have to shop in a specialty store, particularly when you are looking for fresh herbs, unusual spices, and low-fat cheeses. A number of the recipes calling for unusual ingredients suggest substitutes. If you feel you must substitute dried herbs for the fresh (not really recommended), you can do it in the proportions of about one teaspoon dried leaf herbs for one tablespoon fresh chopped herbs.

# GLOSSARY OF KITCHEN EQUIPMENT

In preparing recipes from this cookbook in the New French manner, you will probably have most of the needed equipment in your kitchen already. The recipes have been developed with the average American kitchen in mind. If an item is somewhat unusual, an alternate is often suggested.

Following is a list of equipment helpful in New French Cooking. If the item is essential, that fact is noted; optional items are also noted. This list assumes that you at least have the very basic things: saucepans of various sizes, large and small skillets, mixing bowls, measuring cups and spoons, narrow and wide spatulas, kitchen forks and spoons, rubber scraper, tongs, strainer, baking and roasting pans, casseroles.

**Baster**—Handy to have, the bulb baster is a plastic tube with a tapered tip and a rubber suction bulb at the opposite end. Use it for basting roast poultry and meats with pan juices. Also useful for suctioning fat off the surface of stews, soups, and cooking liquids prior to thickening.

**Beater**—Either a hand-turned rotary beater or a portable electric beater (mixer) is needed, particularly for beating egg whites and whipping. The standing electric mixer is optional, because New French cuisine does not include cakes, cookies, and pastries.

**Blender, electric**—Either a blender or a food processor (see description below) is essential in the New French Cooking to handle the frequent purée-ing. Blenders also can chop, grate, and grind, but function less efficiently than food processors. Foods may need to be handled in small batches; liquid may be needed. (*See* food mill.)

**Casseroles**—Sometimes a confusing term when French recipes are translated. The most common American casseroles cannot be used for top-of-range cookery, as some French casseroles can. Glass or pottery casseroles are best for oven cookery. Enameled cast iron or pyroceram can go from rangetop use to the oven; they are more expensive. Several sizes are useful.

**Chafing dish**—Not necessary, but sometimes nice for entertaining. Liquid or solid fuel is lighted in the underneath container. For keeping buffet foods warm, use the water-bath pan and keep water simmering. For at-the-table cookery, use the upper brazier pan only over the flame.

**Cheesecloth**—Keep several clean pieces handy for straining fine solid particles out of stocks and sauces. More efficient than a fine sieve.

**Clay casseroles**—Not necessary, but fun to use in place of a regular casserole or Dutch oven for long, slow, even cooking of stews, poultry, and less tender meats in the oven. With the lid on, the food braises and mingles flavors with the enclosed liquid and seasonings.

**Colander**—A rounded metal bowl with holes; helpful for draining raw vegetables and fruits after washing and for thorough draining of cooked foods.

**Cutting board**—Necessary to protect counter while slicing, chopping, and dicing. Scrub well after each use. Wood is the most common material, but the new specially designed plastic ones are gaining popularity.

**Double boiler**—A two-part pan with lid. The bottom holds simmering water to slowly cook food in the top and keep it from boiling. Not used often in New French Cooking, but essential for custards and some egg-thickened sauces.

**Dutch oven**—A large round pan of cast iron, cast aluminum, or stainless steel with lid and short handles on either side. Needed for stock, soups, stews, and braised dishes. Can replace soup kettle. Six-quart size handles most needs. Eight- and ten-quart sizes useful when cooking for a crowd.

**Electric blender**—*See* blender.

**Electric mixer/beater**—*See* beater.

**Food mill**—A hand-operated utensil for puréeing foods. The rounded container holds the food, while a disc is rotated manually to press the food through small holes. The food mill is placed over a large bowl to catch the puréed food. Does not do all the many tasks of electric blenders or food processors, but is especially useful for puréeing fruits and vegetables cooked in their skins, such as apples and squash. Most peels do not go through the holes.

**Food processor**—A multi-purpose electric appliance relatively new on the market, which performs many kitchen tasks usually done by separate pieces of equipment, such as grinding, slicing, chopping, puréeing, shredding, and mincing. Food is processed very quickly, due to the high-powered motor. Does what a blender handles and more; blenders do not slice or grind and food must be processed in small batches. Invented in France and recommended by many French chefs.

**Garlic press**—A clamp squeezes the garlic through small holes in the press. Not necessary, but prevents garlicky fingers. No need to peel each clove. (*See* mortar and pestle.)

**Grater**—Useful for hand-grating cheese, carrots, and other vegetables. One type is pyramid-shaped with a different-size hole on each of the four sides; one side slices. Another style is flat, with different-size holes arranged in a series of three or four rows. Necessary if you do not own an electric food processor.

**Juicer**—A small hand model nice for juicing lemons. A bit tedious for quantities of orange juice; attachment on electric mixer would be better. A ridged cone-shaped center holds the fruit; juice drips through holes, while pulp and seeds are trapped behind.

**Knives**—An assortment of sharp knives is necessary in any kitchen. A basic set for French and American cooking would include: a large, wedge-shaped French chopping knife; a long, thin slicing knife; a medium-size utility knife; a serrated-edge bread knife; and a small paring knife. Others nice to have are a curved grapefruit knife, a boning knife, an Oriental curved two-handled rocker for chopping; a smaller wedge-shaped chopping knife. A sharpening steel or electric knife sharpener is essential and should be used often.

**Mallet**—A long-handled wooden utensil helpful for flattening cutlets; those with waffled sides also tenderize. The edge of a pie plate could substitute, but is not as efficient.

**Meat grinder**—Only needed if you do not have a food processor and want to grind meat for sausages, mousses, croquettes, and patties. Can also be used for vegetables and fruits, and for making bread crumbs.

**Molds**—Decorative or shaped molds are elegant for gelatin-based desserts, first courses, and salads. Both individual metal molds or large 4- to 8-cup molds are nice to have.

**Mortar and pestle**—Helpful for crushing spices and herbs or mashing garlic. The mortar is a small round bowl; the pestle does the crushing. Available in wood or ceramic.

**Nonstick finishes**—These come under several trademarked names and are used on cookware and bakeware. Helpful on skillets for New French cookery because no fat is needed. Food comes out of baking pans without sticking. Some nonstick finishes scratch when used with metal utensils.

**Pepper mill**—Lets you grind whole peppercorns as you need pepper in cooking or at the table. Freshly ground pepper is essential in New French Cooking.

**Ramekins**—Individual baking dishes which are attractive enough to go to the table, yet withstand oven heat.

**Salad basket**—Salad greens are placed inside after washing, and much of the water can easily be shaken out.

**Skewers**—Pointed metal utensils which are of several types. The shorter kitchen variety is needed for enclosing stuffings in meat and poultry. The long type is used for kabobs; sometimes these are decorative.

**Skimmer**—A long-handled shallow spoon used in removing fat from liquids, a necessary step in New French Cooking. A bulb baster or large kitchen spoon may also be used.

**Soufflé dish**—A straight-sided baking dish usually made of glazed pottery, used for baked or refrigerator soufflés and some mousses.

**Spice mill**—Electric or hand operated, it is needed if you choose to freshly grind whole spices.

**Steamer, fish or vegetable**—The long metal fish steamer has a perforated basket for holding fish up out of the boiling liquid. Not essential, but nice if you do a lot of fish cookery. Vegetable steamers are of various types and useful if you prefer the full flavor of steamed vegetables. One kind fits inside a large saucepan and fans out to fit the pan being used. Another is like the top of a double boiler, but with a perforated bottom. Not essential, because vegetables can be simmered in water or stock.

**Strainer**—A utensil made of fine wire mesh, needed for straining. Can also be used for puréeing, when food is pushed through with a wooden spoon.

**Thermometer**—A meat thermometer is essential for gauging the exact doneness of meat. New French cuisine meats should be cooked just to the right point; further roasting makes the meat or poultry dry out, toughen, and lose flavor. Candy and deep-fat-frying thermometers are not needed because this kind of cooking is not done in the New French cuisine.

**Tongs**—Metal or wooden tongs are needed to lift large pieces of food from hot cooking liquid.

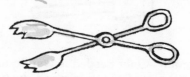

**Wire whip**—A rounded, balloon-shaped utensil with a wire coil handle and a series of overlapping wires in the rounded end. Used often by the French for beating egg whites, folding in egg whites, whipping, and stirring sauces.

**Wok**—A large bowl-shaped pan used in Chinese cooking, primarily for quick stir-frying.

## GLOSSARY OF METHODS AND TERMS

The following list does not include all cooking methods, terms, and ingredients used in this book of New French Cooking. What it does provide is a brief definition of the more unusual ingredients and terms, as well as some procedures particularly common to the new cuisine. Familiar cooking methods may have a new twist to eliminate fat and lighten the finished dish.

**Arrowroot**—A thickener used frequently in this book. It has the same thickening power as cornstarch; sauces are more delicate in texture. One tablespoon thickens one cup liquid to medium consistency. Arrowroot sauces do not hold long; if you wish a dish to wait before serving, use cornstarch.

**Beating egg whites**—Use very clean, dry equipment. Separate egg yolks from whites very carefully. Have egg whites at room temperature. Beat with a rotary beater or electric mixer. Add a little cream of tartar or salt for stability. Sugar is reduced or eliminated in New French Cooking. Beat until peaks do not fall over, but do not let whites become dry.

**Bouquet garni**—A bundle of several sprigs of parsley, a sprig of fresh thyme, and a bay leaf tied with string for flavoring cooking liquids. Discard before serving.

**Braising**—A method of slowly simmering food in a covered utensil on top of the range or in the oven. It tenderizes the tougher cuts of meat and is excellent for cooking poultry, because the enclosed cooking lets the flavors and aromas mingle. In New French Cooking the meat or poultry is not browned first in fat.

**Cheese**—Generally, the cheeses used in New French Cooking are those low in fat. This means taking care in selection because the vast majority of all cheeses on the market are high-fat. Recipes in this book use low-fat ricotta, low-fat cottage cheese (it can substitute for ricotta; or you can drain the cream off regular cottage cheese), Jarlsberg (like Swiss cheese but lower in fat), Neufchatel, and pot cheese. Higher-fat Swiss and Cheddar are used sparingly in a few recipes. Look for low-fat cheeses of other types in your market. Cheeses and, of course, milk are the primary sources of the important nutrient calcium.

**Chilies, green**—A rather spicy Mexican pepper. Available fresh in some markets, but more available in cans.

**Chill**—Place in refrigerator until cold.

**Chop**—To cut up in irregular pieces with a knife or chopper, either coarsely (¼- to ½-inch pieces) or finely (⅛- to ¼-inch pieces).

**Clarified butter**—Butter with the milk solids removed. Melt butter over low heat. Tilt pan; skim foam from top and spoon clear butter off, leaving residue in pan. It is used because milk solids tend to burn before the butter is hot.

**Cool**—Let stand at room temperature until no longer warm.

**Crème fraîche**—A classic French ingredient for sauces and soups which gives body and rich creaminess. Real crème fraîche is a heavy cream fermented naturally to a very thick product, somewhat tart and nutlike in flavor. It is very high in calories and fat. Available commercially in some markets; expensive. A mock crème fraîche has been developed for use in recipes in this book; see the Sauces and Stocks chapter.

**Degrease**—To skim or remove fat that rises to the surface of a cooking liquid. The easiest method is to chill the liquid until the fat solidifies; then lift it off. With hot liquids, spoon the fat from the surface or use a bulb baster to siphon it off.

**Dice**—To cut into small cubes, about ¼ inch.

**Dijon mustard**—A spicy mustard from Dijon, France. Because it is made with wine, substitutes are not quite the same.

**Fold**—A method of gently combining beaten egg whites or whipped nonfat dry milk (whipped cream is not used in New French Cooking) with another heavier mixture. Heap beaten whites or milk on top. Pass a wire whip or rubber spatula down through entire contents and across the bottom; bring up some of the lower portion to the surface. Continue gently until evenly combined.

**Fruit concentrates**—Natural concentrates of various fruits such as peach, apple, blackberry, and strawberry. Available in specialty sections of supermarkets or gourmet food stores. When used in dessert recipes, sugar is usually not needed.

**Grind**—To put food through some type of grinding equipment to reduce it to fine particles, as in grinding meats. A hand or electric meat grinder may be used, or an electric food processor or blender. Pepper and spices are also ground in special mills.

**Herbs**—Fresh herbs are best for New French Cooking. Grow your own or purchase at specialty stores. If you must substitute dry herbs, use about ½ the quantity of fresh, sometimes less. Use ¼ to ⅓ as much of ground dry herbs.

**Julienne**—To cut meat or vegetables into thin, matchlike strips.

**Liquids for cooking**—Water has no flavor, so whenever possible use stock (meat, poultry, fish, vegetable) and/or wine.

**Marinate**—To let a food stand in a liquid for a period of time, usually in the refrigerator, so the food can take on the flavor of the liquid. Wine, vinegar, or lemon juice is usually used along with such flavorings as onions, herbs, and spices. The liquid is called the marinade.

**Mince**—To chop very finely, ⅛-inch pieces or less.

**Poach**—To cook food in a simmering liquid in a covered utensil. Often used for fish and eggs.

**Purée**—A procedure common in New French recipes. Food is pressed through a food mill, strainer, or sieve or processed in an electric blender or food processor until it is in a pulpy state, like a thick liquid. Puréed vegetables often thicken sauces and soups; puréed fruits flavor desserts and often eliminate the need for sugar.

**Reduce**—To boil down a cooking liquid to lessen its volume and thereby concentrate the flavor and thicken slightly. Used in some New French recipes in place of a flour thickener.

**Roast**—To cook meat or poultry in the oven, uncovered. Should be used only with tender cuts of meat; tough cuts should be covered and braised.

**Sauté**—An old French method of cooking a food in hot fat, stirring frequently. Often used with chopped onions, celery, and mushrooms. Sautéeing is not done in New French Cooking, nor is frying. Instead onions, celery, and mushrooms are simmered in stock or wine. The skillet should be uncovered to allow desirable volatile flavors to escape, particularly with onions.

**Shallots**—A small member of the onion family with a mellow flavor. Larger than green onions. A dry type of onion. Used often in France; not very plentiful in the U.S.

**Simmer**—To cook just below boiling point, about 185°F. Liquid bubbles around the edges, but not throughout.

**Skewer**—To hold in place with a metal or wooden skewer, as with stuffings inside meat and poultry.

**Skim fat**—*See* degrease.

**Soybeans; soy grits**—Used more often in Middle and Far Eastern cooking. Available in health food stores. Undesirable in flavor when served plain, but can be interesting when combined with other foods.

**Soy sauce, light**—Used in Chinese cooking. Less pungent than dark soy sauce.

**Steam**—To cook a food over boiling water, rather than in the liquid. See equipment section for steamers. Steamed food is often fuller in flavor. Food may also be steamed by wrapping in foil and baking.

**Szechuan pepper**—Spicy pepper from the Szechuan province of China. Available in specialty stores and Chinese shops. Should be lightly roasted in a skillet just before grinding for use. Used in many non-Oriental recipes in this book because of its special flavor.

**Thickeners**—In true New French Cooking, flour does not thicken sauces. It adds some extra calories and detracts from the sauce flavor. In this book many recipes use delicate arrowroot, reduction of liquids, and puréed vegetable or fruit ingredients. Sauces will not be as thick as standard American gravy.

**Unmolding**—To unmold a gelatin dish, run a knife along edge; dip 15 to 20 seconds in very hot water. Place inverted platter over mold; quickly flip over. Food should slip out. If unsuccessful, dip in hot water a few seconds more.

**Yogurt**—A fermented milk product which is acidic and is thick enough to spoon. Available commercially in many flavors. If purchasing for use in these recipes, always buy plain low-fat yogurt, unsweetened and unflavored—not even vanilla. You can make your own with the recipe in the Sauces and Stocks chapter.

# SAUCES AND STOCKS

Chilled Artichoke Plate, 31; Cucumber Sauce, 21;
Individual Chicken Terrines, 29

Without basic stocks and a large repertory of standardized, well-established sauces there would be no classic French cuisine. Béarnaise, hollandaise, mayonnaise, Mornay, velouté, Bordelaise, béchamel, demiglace, buttersauce, and dozens more are world renowned, and every good chef prepares them in the same manner.

Sauces and stocks are significant in the new style of French cooking, too, as they add glamour to everyday foods. However, the new cooking does not set any particular requirements for how sauces must be made—only that they should be light and relatively low in fat. The chef or home cook is free to experiment, the main limits being the boundaries of fine taste and the creativity of the mind.

Sauces may either be prepared separately or from a dish's cooking liquid. The latter method is used less frequently in classic cooking. This chapter gives a collection of sauces prepared separately, usually with a stock or vegetable base. They may be used on meat, fish, poultry, or vegetables, and recipes in other chapters use them as ingredients. Some of the sauce recipes are our lightened versions of popular classic sauces.

The sauces in this chapter use no butter or flour. They are given body or a slight thickness with a little arrowroot (which is more delicate than cornstarch or flour, although cornstarch has the same thickening power and can be substituted) or by puréeing vegetables.

Sauces are made creamy in several light and in-genious ways: with low-fat ricotta or cottage cheese, yogurt, low-fat milk, or with our version of Mock Crème Fraîche. Except for the milk, these also thicken the sauce.

True crème fraîche is a heavy cream which is fermented naturally into a product which is very rich, thick, and nutlike in flavor. It is now available commercially in some U.S. markets, but it is loaded with calories and very expensive. Our version has about one half the calories of the commercial product; it is made with yogurt and ricotta cheese. Crème fraîche gives creamy body to sauces and salad dressings and will not curdle.

The three basic stock recipes in this chapter will be used in a myriad of ways throughout this book, especially the chicken and beef stocks. They are nice to have on hand in your refrigerator or freezer. They are used as a base for sauces, as cooking liquids in stews and braised dishes, for cooking vegetables, mock "sautéeing" of onions and mushrooms, in soups, and even in vinaigrette salad dressing and a vegetable mousse.

Stocks are made pretty much as they are for classic cooking, except that the meat is not browned in fat and the stock is not reduced as greatly, thus shortening the cooking time. Stocks should be refrigerated after cooking; the fat will rise to the surface and solidify for easy removal. For recipes in this book it is not necessary to clarify the stocks. Good quality canned stocks and extracts can be used in place of the homemade versions.

## Mock Crème Fraîche

*Crème fraîche is a heavy cream which is fermented naturally. It is very thick and nutlike in flavor and is used in French cooking to give body to sauces. Unlike sour cream, it will not curdle when cooked. Crème fraîche has recently become available in this country; it is very high in calories and very expensive. Our version has half the calories and is simple and inexpensive to make.*

**1½ cups Neufchatel cheese**
**6 tablespoons Low-Fat Yogurt**
**(page 19)**

1. Mix cheese and yogurt in a blender or food processor until smooth and fluffy. Place in small jars; cover tightly.
2. Set jars in a warm place (100° to 125°F) for 2 hours; see Note. Cool and refrigerate. Stir before using.

*About 2 cups*

*Note:* Use an oven thermometer in making Mock Crème Fraîche, as temperature is very important. A gas oven with a pilot light will be about 125°F. Turn electric oven to as warm a setting as necessary to maintain temperature. Mock Crème Fraîche can be refrigerated up to 3 weeks.

# Low-Fat Yogurt

1 quart 2% milk
¼ cup instant nonfat dry-milk
     solids
2 tablespoons low-fat natural
     yogurt

1. Mix milk and dry-milk solids in a medium saucepan. Heat to scalding (150°F); cool to 110°F. Stir in yogurt.
2. Transfer mixture to a glass or crockery bowl. Cover with plastic wrap; wrap bowl securely in a heavy bath towel. Set in a warm place (100° to 125°F)* for 4 to 6 hours, until yogurt has formed.
3. Place several layers of paper toweling directly on yogurt; refrigerate covered until cold.

*About 1 quart*

*A gas oven with a pilot light will be about 125°F; however, use an oven thermometer, as temperature is very important. Turn an electric oven to as warm a setting as necessary to maintain temperature.

Excess liquid and a coarse texture will result if temperature is too high. Liquid can be drained with a nylon baster. Blend yogurt in a food processor or blender to restore texture.

*Note:* This recipe can be made using skim or reconstituted dry milk, although the product will not be as rich.

Purchased low-fat natural yogurt can be substituted in any recipe.

# Avocado Sauce

*Mexican guacamole was the idea behind this flavorful sauce.*

2 medium avocados, peeled and
     chopped
1 small pared zucchini, chopped
1 tablespoon minced onion
2 teaspoons lemon juice
¼ teaspoon chili powder
1 small tomato, seeded and
     chopped
¼ teaspoon salt

1. Purée avocados, zucchini, onion, lemon juice, and chili powder in a food processor or blender; stir in tomato and salt. Refrigerate covered until chilled (about 1 hour).
2. Serve over pork, veal, poultry, fish, or vegetable salads.

*About 3 cups*

# Cauliflower Sauce

*This sauce has a rich, creamy texture and lends itself well to any recipe calling for a white sauce.*

¾ pound cauliflower
     Chicken Stock (page 25)
½ teaspoon salt
¼ teaspoon freshly ground white
     pepper
2 tablespoons dry white wine
1 teaspoon snipped fresh or ½
     teaspoon dried thyme leaves
2 ounces Swiss cheese, shredded
     Snipped parsley (optional)

1. Remove leaves and tough stalks from cauliflower; separate into flowerets. Simmer cauliflower, covered, in 1 inch of stock until tender (about 8 minutes); drain.
2. Purée cauliflower with remaining ingredients, except cheese and parsley, in a food processor or blender. Heat thoroughly over low heat. Stir in cheese; heat, stirring constantly, until cheese is melted (about 2 minutes).
3. Stir parsley into sauce, if desired, and serve immediately as a sauce or soup.

*About 1⅓ cups*

# Garlic-Parsley Sauce

*Garlic cloves lose their pungency and develop a delicate flavor when poached. Flavors of garlic, mushrooms, green onion, and parsley merge in this hearty sauce.*

30 large garlic cloves, peeled
  Water
¾ cup Chicken Stock (page 25)
1½ cups sliced fresh mushrooms
1 teaspoon minced green onion
1 tablespoon snipped parsley
¼ teaspoon salt
½ teaspoon bottled brown
  bouquet sauce

1. Cover garlic cloves with water in a saucepan; heat to boiling and drain. Repeat 2 more times. Add remaining ingredients, except brown bouquet sauce, to garlic in saucepan; simmer, covered, 15 minutes.
2. Purée all ingredients and brown bouquet sauce in a food processor or blender. Heat in a saucepan to serve hot, or refrigerate and serve cold.
3. Serve on roast beef, steak, or veal. Or fill **mushroom caps** with sauce; bake at 300°F 15 minutes.

*About 2 cups*

*Note:* Substitute ¼ cup stock for red wine, if desired.

# Seasoned Dark Green Sauce

*1 pound spinach, washed and
  stems removed
1 teaspoon anchovy paste
1 large garlic clove, minced
1 drop Tabasco
1 tablespoon instant nonfat
  dry-milk solids
¾ to 1 cup Chicken Stock (page
  25)

1. Simmer spinach with water clinging to leaves in a covered saucepan until spinach is tender (about 7 minutes); drain.
2. Purée in a food processor or blender with remaining ingredients, adding amount of stock necessary for a medium sauce consistency. Heat in a saucepan to serve hot or refrigerate to serve cold.
3. Serve over poultry, fish, or cooked vegetables. Or serve as a vegetable in small bowls and top with yogurt.

*About 2 cups*

*1 package (10 ounces) frozen leaf spinach can be used. Cook according to package instructions; drain well.

# Green Peppercorn Sauce

*Green peppercorns are the whole unripe berries from the pepper vine. They are generally processed and packed in brine. Their pungent flavor makes this a distinctive sauce.*

1 cup Chicken Stock (page 25)
2 tablespoons brandy
1 tablespoon arrowroot
  Cold water
¼ pound fresh mushrooms,
  chopped
¼ cup Mock Crème Fraîche (page
  18)
½ teaspoon salt
¼ teaspoon freshly ground
  pepper
2 tablespoons drained green
  peppercorns

1. Heat stock and brandy.
2. Mix arrowroot with a little cold water; stir into stock. Simmer, stirring constantly, until stock has thickened (about 4 minutes). Stir in remaining ingredients. Heat thoroughly. Serve immediately.

*About 2½ cups*

# Light Green Sauce

1 cup finely chopped lettuce
   Peel of 1 large zucchini
¼ cup parsley sprigs, stems
   removed
1 tablespoon chopped green
   onion
⅔ cup low-fat ricotta cheese
¾ teaspoon salt
⅛ teaspoon freshly ground white
   pepper
2 teaspoons fresh lemon juice
⅓ to ½ cup Chicken Stock (page
   25)

1. Purée all ingredients in a food processor or blender, adding amount of stock necessary for a medium sauce consistency.
2. Serve over hot or cold vegetables, poached fish, or chicken.

*About 1¼ cups*

# Artichoke Sauce

*This sauce is so elegant in flavor that you would never guess it is so easy to make.*

1 can (8 ounces) artichoke hearts,
   cut in quarters
¼ cup low-fat ricotta cheese
⅓ to ½ cup Chicken Stock (page
   25)
¼ teaspoon salt
⅛ teaspoon freshly ground white
   pepper

1. Purée all ingredients in a food processor or blender, adding more stock if necessary for a fairly thick consistency. Heat in a saucepan to serve hot, or refrigerate and serve cold.
2. Serve with veal, pork, fish, vegetables, or eggs.

*About 1½ cups*

*Note:* To serve as a soup, add more stock to sauce for desired consistency.

# Cucumber Sauce

1 medium cucumber, pared,
   seeded, and finely chopped
   Chicken Stock (page 25)
1½ cups Low-Fat Yogurt (page 19)
1 tablespoon snipped fresh or
   1½ teaspoons dried dill
   weed
¼ teaspoon salt
   Dash freshly ground white
   pepper

1. Simmer cucumber in 1 inch of stock in a covered saucepan until tender (about 5 minutes); drain off and discard stock.
2. Mix cucumbers with remaining ingredients. Serve cold, or heat and serve warm.

*About 2 cups*

*Note:* Snipped coriander or mint can be used in place of dill in this recipe.

# Cumberland Sauce

½ cup fresh cranberries
2 teaspoons grated orange peel
1 large navel orange, peeled and finely chopped
2 tablespoons brandy
½ cup port wine
¼ cup orange juice
¼ cup Beef Stock (page 25)
1 teaspoon prepared mustard

1. Process cranberries, orange peel and chopped orange, and brandy in a food processor or blender until finely ground.
2. Transfer mixture to a saucepan; stir in remaining ingredients. Simmer uncovered until sauce is of medium thick consistency (about 15 minutes). Serve hot, or refrigerate and serve cold.
3. Serve over duck, pork, ham, or over cottage cheese or fruit salads.

*About 1½ cups*

# Mock Hollandaise Sauce

*Our recipe boasts one-third the calories of the traditional hollandaise sauce. It has an enjoyable, smooth texture and tart flavor with no butter or egg yolks added.*

½ cup Neufchatel cheese
3 tablespoons Low-Fat Yogurt (page 19)
Dash salt
Juice of ½ lemon

1. Mix all ingredients in a blender or food processor until smooth and fluffy.
2. Cook over simmering water until hot and thickened. Serve immediately or refrigerate and serve cold. Stir before using.

*¾ cup*

**Mock Béarnaise Sauce:** Stir **1½ teaspoons snipped fresh** or **½ teaspoon dried tarragon leaves** and **½ teaspoon minced shallots** into sauce before heating.

**Mock Mayonnaise:** Stir **1½ teaspoons Dijon mustard** and **½ teaspoon sugar** into sauce before heating. Refrigerate until cold.

*Note:* The above sauces can be refrigerated up to 3 weeks.

# Herbed Mock Mayonnaise

*Mock Mayonnaise given a new flavor twist can be used as a sauce, a salad dressing, or a dip for raw vegetables.*

1 cup Mock Mayonnaise (page 22)
2 teaspoons snipped fresh or 1 teaspoon dried crumbled tarragon leaves
2 teaspoons snipped fresh chervil or parsley
½ garlic clove, minced
½ teaspoon minced onion

Mix all ingredients. Refrigerate 3 hours or overnight. Stir before serving.

*1 cup*

# Citrus Mayonnaise

    1 cup Mock Mayonnaise (page
      22)
    1 tablespoon fresh orange juice
    1 tablespoon fresh lemon juice
    1 teaspoon grated orange peel
      Dash ground white pepper

Mix all ingredients in a small bowl. Refrigerate covered ½ hour. Stir before serving.

*About 1 cup*

# Madeira Sauce

    1 cup Chicken Stock (page 25)
      Juice of 1 lemon
    1 teaspoon Worcestershire sauce
    ¼ teaspoon salt
    ⅓ cup Madeira wine
    1 tablespoon arrowroot
      Cold water
    1 tablespoon snipped parsley

1. Heat stock, lemon juice, Worcestershire sauce, salt, and Madeira in a small saucepan.
2. Mix arrowroot with a little cold water; stir into stock mixture. Simmer, stirring constantly, until thickened (about 3 minutes). Stir in parsley. Serve immediately.

*About 1½ cups*

# Savory Tomato Sauce

    5 large tomatoes, peeled, cored,
      and coarsely chopped
    ⅔ cup chopped green onions
    ⅔ cup chopped celery
    1 large green pepper, cored and
      chopped
    2 tablespoons snipped parsley
    ¾ cup tomato juice
    ½ teaspoon cumin
    ¼ teaspoon chili powder
    ¼ teaspoon garlic powder
    ⅛ teaspoon ground cloves
    1½ teaspoons salt

Mix all ingredients in a 3-quart saucepan. Simmer uncovered until sauce is of medium, not thick, consistency (about 1 hour).

*About 1 quart*

# Green Onion Sauce

    2 bunches green onions, sliced
    1 medium zucchini, cut in 1-inch
      pieces
    1½ to 1⅔ cups Chicken Stock
      (page 25)
    ½ teaspoon salt

1. Simmer onions and zucchini in 1½ cups stock in a covered saucepan until tender (about 10 minutes).
2. Purée vegetables, stock, and salt in a food processor or blender, adding more stock if necessary for a medium sauce consistency. Heat in a saucepan to serve hot, or refrigerate and serve cold.
3. Serve over cooked vegetables, roast beef, pork, or lamb, or as a dip for raw vegetables.

*About 2 cups*

*Note:* To serve as a cold soup, thin with ½ cup stock and top with a **dollop of yogurt.**

## Middle Eastern Sauce

1 cup raw soybeans
3 cups water
1 teaspoon salt
½ cup Low-Fat Yogurt (page 19)
1 teaspoon cumin
½ teaspoon sesame or vegetable oil
¼ teaspoon curry powder
1 teaspoon minced garlic
¼ to ½ teaspoon salt

1. Simmer soybeans in water with 1 teaspoon salt in a covered saucepan 3 hours; drain, reserving ½ cup liquid.
2. Purée soybeans with remaining ingredients in a food processor or blender; add reserved liquid as necessary for a medium sauce consistency.
3. Serve warm over steamed vegetables, chicken, or lamb. Or refrigerate until chilled and serve as a dip for assorted vegetables.

*About 2½ cups*

## Vinaigrette Dressing

*Chicken stock replaces most of the oil in this recipe. Great as a sauce, salad dressing, or marinade.*

1 tablespoon fresh lemon juice
1 tablespoon olive or vegetable oil
¼ cup Chicken Stock (page 25)
2 teaspoons snipped parsley
1 teaspoon snipped fresh or
½ teaspoon dried basil leaves
2 teaspoons distilled white vinegar
1 teaspoon Dijon mustard
1 small garlic clove, minced
⅛ teaspoon salt
Freshly ground white pepper

Measure all ingredients into a jar with a tight cover; shake vigorously. Refrigerate dressing until chilled. Shake before serving.

*About ½ cup*

## White Vegetable Purée

*You will enjoy the rich texture of this hearty sauce—puréed turnips and potatoes form the base.*

¾ pound white potatoes, pared and cut in 1-inch pieces
¾ pound turnips, pared and cut in 1-inch pieces
Water
¼ cup instant nonfat dry-milk solids
½ cup 2% milk
1 teaspoon salt
¼ teaspoon freshly ground white pepper
1 tablespoon clarified butter
¼ to ⅓ cup Mock Crème Fraîche (page 18), if desired

1. Simmer potatoes and turnips in 1½ inches water in a large covered saucepan until tender (about 20 minutes). Drain vegetables; reserve cooking liquid.
2. Purée vegetables with milk solids, milk, salt, pepper, and butter in a food processor or blender. Add reserved cooking liquid and Mock Crème Fraîche, if used, for desired consistency. Return mixture to saucepan and heat thoroughly.

*About 2 cups*

*Note:* This recipe can be served as a soup if thinned with skim milk.

# Custard Sauce

1 cup Low-Fat Yogurt (page 19)
1 egg yolk
2 teaspoons honey or apple
    concentrate

Beat all ingredients until fluffy. Serve immediately or refrigerate until chilled.

*About 1 ¼ cups*

# Beef Stock

1 pound lean beef stew cubes
1 pound lean veal stew cubes
½ pound beef soup bones
3 carrots, cut in 2-inch pieces
1 tomato, quartered and seeded
2 medium yellow onions,
    quartered
1 stalk celery,
    cut in 2-inch pieces
1 garlic clove, minced
1 teaspoon salt
  Bouquet garni:
    ½ teaspoon dried thyme
      leaves
    1 bay leaf
    2 sprigs parsley
  Water

1. Place meats, vegetables, garlic, salt, and bouquet garni in an 8-quart Dutch oven. Pour in water to cover (about 3 quarts). Simmer covered 2 to 2½ hours. Cool slightly.
2. Strain stock through a double thickness of cheesecloth into a storage container. Taste for seasoning. If a more concentrated flavor is desired, return stock to saucepan and simmer 20 to 30 minutes, or dissolve **1 to 2 teaspoons instant beef bouillon** in the stock.
3. Store covered in refrigerator or freezer. Remove solidified fat from top of stock before using.

*2 to 2½ quarts*

*Note:* Refrigerated stock is perishable. If not used within several days, heat to boiling, cool, and refrigerate or freeze to prevent spoilage. Stock can be kept frozen up to 4 months.

# Chicken Stock

5 pounds chicken backs and
    wings, or stewing chicken,
    cut up
3 carrots, cut in 2-inch pieces
2 medium yellow onions,
    quartered
1 stalk celery, cut in 2-inch
    pieces
2 teaspoons salt
  Bouquet garni:
    ¾ teaspoon dried thyme
      leaves
    ¾ teaspoon dried rosemary
      leaves
    1 bay leaf
    4 sprigs parsley
    2 whole cloves
  Water

1. Place chicken, vegetables, salt, and bouquet garni in an 8-quart Dutch oven. Pour in water to cover (about 4 quarts). Simmer covered 2 to 2½ hours.
2. Strain stock through a double thickness of cheesecloth into a storage container. Taste for seasoning. If more concentrated flavor is desired, return stock to saucepan and simmer 20 to 30 minutes, or dissolve 1 to 2 teaspoons instant chicken bouillon in the stock.
3. Store covered in refrigerator or freezer. Remove solidified fat from top of stock before using.

*3 to 3½ quarts*

*Note:* Refrigerated stock is perishable. If not used within several days, heat to boiling, cool, and refrigerate or freeze to prevent spoilage. Stock can be kept frozen up to 4 months.

# Fish Stock

2 pounds fresh lean fish with
    heads and bones, cut up
1 medium yellow onion,
    quartered
½ teaspoon salt
1 cup dry white wine
  Bouquet garni:
    4 sprigs parsley
    1 bay leaf
    ½ teaspoon dried thyme
      leaves
    1 sprig celery leaves
    2 peppercorns
  Water

1. Rinse fish under cold water. Place fish, onion, salt, wine, and bouquet garni in a 3-quart saucepan. Pour in water to cover (about 1½ quarts). Simmer covered 2 hours. Cool slightly.
2. Strain stock through a double thickness of cheesecloth into a storage container. Taste for seasoning. Add a small amount of salt and lemon juice, if desired. If a more concentrated flavor is desired, return stock to saucepan and simmer 30 to 45 minutes.
3. Store covered in refrigerator or freezer.

*About 1 quart*

*Note:* Use white firm-fleshed fish such as halibut, cod, flounder, or lemon sole. Frozen fish can be used if necessary.
    Refrigerated stock is highly perishable. If not used within 2 days, heat to boiling, cool, and refrigerate or freeze to prevent spoilage. Stock can be kept frozen up to 2 months.

# Canned Stock

6 cups canned chicken or beef
    bouillon or clam juice
2 medium carrots, cut in 2-inch
    pieces
2 medium onions, peeled and
    quartered
¾ cup dry white wine, if desired
  Bouquet garni:
    4 sprigs parsley
    2 bay leaves
    1 teaspoon dried thyme
      leaves

1. Combine all ingredients in a 2-quart saucepan. Simmer covered 45 minutes.
2. Strain stock through a double thickness of cheesecloth into a storage container. Refrigerate.

*About 1½ quarts*

# FIRST COURSES AND APPETIZERS

Lighter meals mean fewer courses. Hence, those grand meals that begin with an appetizer and end six courses later with a sumptuous dessert, demitasse, and cognac are ostentatious and passé, believe the followers of the New French cuisine. And with fewer courses, you do not eat an appetizer *and* a soup *and* a fish course before the entrée.

Therefore, this chapter on first courses includes a variety of foods that could open the meal. It might be a traditional but light appetizer, *or* a non-rich soup, *or* small portions of a fish dish (see pages 50–56). You could even serve the salad or vegetable dish as a first course. (With a classic menu the salad would follow the meat course.) For a special occasion you could certainly serve a light appetizer *and* a light soup, but on a daily-meal basis the shorter menu would be preferable.

Do serve a first course; it is very French. Even with the smaller meals of the new cuisine, the tradition of multicourse meals has not been abandoned. It is an elegant, relaxing, enjoyable way to dine.

Within the concept of the healthier form of eating, cocktail hour hors d'oeuvres and other nibbling foods should be eliminated. They add too many extra calories and lessen the enjoyment of the meal you have taken such care to create. A planned first course at the table controls the amount of food eaten and is really more elegant. If you insist, serve *crudités*—an array of colorful raw vegetables.

The potent American cocktail is also out of place preceding any style of French meal. A glass of white wine, champagne, dry sherry, an apéritif wine such as lillet, or kir (white wine with crème de cassis) would be more appropriate.

# Liver Pâté

*This is not baked, but made with gelatin and chilled. Calories can be cut by serving with vegetables rather than the usual crackers.*

1½ cups chopped onion
1 cup chopped celery
1½ cups Chicken Stock (page 25)
1 cup dry white wine
1 teaspoon paprika
⅛ teaspoon ground allspice or cloves
¼ teaspoon garlic powder
4 drops Tabasco
1¼ teaspoons salt
1½ pounds chicken livers, membranes removed
2 envelopes unflavored gelatin
½ cup cold water
Assorted vegetable relishes

1. Simmer onion and celery in stock and wine in an uncovered saucepan until liquid is reduced to 2 cups (about 15 minutes). Stir in paprika, allspice, garlic powder, Tabasco, and salt; simmer 2 minutes. Stir in livers; simmer covered until livers are tender (about 15 minutes). Drain; discard liquid.
2. Sprinkle gelatin over cold water; let stand 3 minutes. Set over low heat, stirring occasionally, until gelatin is dissolved (about 5 minutes).
3. Purée half the livers and vegetables along with half the gelatin mixture in a food processor or blender. Repeat with remaining ingredients; combine the two mixtures.
4. Pour mixture into a lightly oiled 1½-quart mold or bowl or ten 6-ounce custard cups. Chill until set (about 4 hours).
5. Serve from mold, or unmold onto platter and accompany with assorted vegetables.

*10 to 12 servings*

# Tangerine Yakatori

*This colorful Japanese-style appetizer is as pleasing to the eye as it is to the taste.*

½ cup tangerine or orange juice
¼ cup dry white wine
3 tablespoons light soy sauce
½ bunch green onions, cut in 1-inch pieces
2 large tangerines or oranges, peeled, sectioned, and seeded
2 large whole chicken breasts, skinned, boned, and cut in 1x¼-inch strips

1. Combine all ingredients in a mixing bowl. Refrigerate covered 2 hours, stirring occasionally. Drain; reserve marinade.
2. Thread ingredients alternately on wooden skewers. Broil 4 inches from heat until chicken is done (about 3 minutes on each side).
3. Heat marinade until bubbly. Serve in individual cups as a dipping sauce.

*4 servings*

# Individual Chicken Terrines

*Crisp carrots and the delicate flavor of brandy enliven this appetizing dish.*

½ cup thinly sliced small carrots
¼ cup brandy
2 pounds boned chicken, coarsely chopped
1 small onion
1 small carrot
1 teaspoon salt
¼ teaspoon nutmeg
1 egg, lightly beaten
2 teaspoons vegetable oil
2 tablespoons ice water
1½ tablespoons matzo meal or white cornmeal
Vegetable oil
Watercress
Cucumber Sauce (page 21), if desired

1. Simmer carrot slices in brandy in a covered saucepan just until tender (about 3 minutes). Remove carrots with a slotted spoon; reserve. Mix a quarter of the chicken with brandy; remove from heat and let stand 45 minutes. Drain.
2. Mince remaining chicken, the onion, and carrot in a food processor or blender; remove to a mixing bowl. Stir in marinated chicken, salt, nutmeg, egg, oil, and ice water; mix well. Sprinkle matzo meal over mixture; mix well.
3. Layer the carrot slices in bottom of 8 lightly oiled 6-ounce custard cups. Spoon chicken mixture over carrots, smoothing top of mixture. Cover cups tightly with aluminum foil; place in a baking pan. Pour boiling water into baking pan, halfway up sides of custard cups.
4. Bake at 325°F 40 to 45 minutes, or until mixture is set. Remove cups from water. Remove foil. Let stand 5 minutes.
5. Terrines can be served hot, or refrigerated until chilled and served cold. To unmold, run knife around edge of cups and invert on individual plates. Garnish with watercress. Serve with Cucumber Sauce, if desired.

*8 servings*

*Note:* For a luncheon entrée, follow directions above, using six 10-ounce glass dishes. Bake until mixture is set.

# Crab Meat and Bean Sprouts with Omelet Strips

2 eggs
3 tablespoons water
1 tablespoon dry sherry
1 tablespoon light soy sauce
1 tablespoon walnut or vegetable oil
4 green onions, chopped
¾ cup chopped green pepper
1 cup sliced fresh mushrooms
2 cups drained fresh or canned bean sprouts
1 tablespoon light soy sauce
8 ounces fresh or 1 can (7¾ ounces) crab meat, drained and flaked
1 teaspoon toasted sesame seed

1. Beat eggs with water, sherry, and 1 tablespoon soy sauce. Heat half the walnut oil in a small skillet. Cook egg mixture in skillet until set but still moist on top; remove to plate and cut egg into strips.
2. Heat remaining walnut oil in a wok or medium skillet. Cook and stir vegetables and 1 tablespoon soy sauce until vegetables are just tender (about 3 minutes). Add crab meat and omelet strips; cook and stir until thoroughly heated (about 1 minute). Sprinkle with toasted sesame seed. Serve immediately.

*4 servings*

## Oysters in Mushroom Purée

1 pound mushrooms, coarsely
  chopped
1 quart oysters, liquor reserved
¼ cup dry sherry
½ cup soft bread crumbs
2 garlic cloves, minced
1 teaspoon salt
¼ teaspoon freshly ground
  pepper
  Beef Stock (page 25)
  Watercress

1. Simmer mushrooms and 1 cup of the oysters in the sherry in a covered saucepan 8 to 10 minutes. Drain; press all moisture out of mushrooms.
2. Purée mushrooms and cooked oysters in a food processor or blender; pour into a shallow 1½-quart casserole. Stir in the bread crumbs, garlic, salt, and pepper. Stir in reserved oyster liquor. Stir in stock, if necessary, to make purée of a thick sauce consistency. Arrange remaining oysters in purée.
3. Bake covered at 350°F 20 minutes.
4. Serve in shallow bowls or ramekins. Garnish with watercress.

*6 to 8 servings*

## Broiled Fish Quenelles

*The traditional method of poaching is given along with our new, easy broiling method. The quenelles puff to a light texture when cooked.*

2 pounds skinned fish fillets (all
  trout or a combination of
  trout, whitefish, or pike)
½ cup chopped onion
⅓ cup chopped carrot
1 egg, beaten
2 teaspoons vegetable oil
1½ teaspoons salt
1½ teaspoons matzo meal or white
  cornmeal
3 tablespoons ice water
  Watercress

1. Place all ingredients except 1 tablespoon of the ice water and watercress in a blender or food processor; purée until the consistency of a paste. Add remaining ice water if necessary (mixture should hold together and be easy to handle).
2. Form fish mixture into oval patties, using ½ cup for each. Place on a lightly oiled cookie sheet.
3. Broil 4 inches from heat until patties are well browned and slightly puffed (8 to 10 minutes on each side). Serve immediately. Garnish with watercress.

*8 servings*

*Note:* Fish quenelles can be poached, if desired. Simmer covered in a large skillet in 1½ quarts Fish Stock (page 26) until puffed and cooked through the center (about 10 minutes). Remove from stock with slotted spoon. Serve hot or refrigerate until chilled. Garnish as above.

# Seviche

*In this specialty of Mexico, the lemon juice actually "cooks" the fish.*

1¼ pounds whitefish fillets,
     skinned and cut in 2x¼-inch
     strips
  1 cup fresh lemon juice
  2 green chilies, seeded and
     minced
  1 teaspoon snipped fresh or ½
     teaspoon dried oregano
     leaves
  1 tablespoon snipped fresh or
     1½ teaspoons dried coriander
     leaves
  1 tablespoon olive oil
  1 teaspoon salt
  ¼ teaspoon freshly ground
     pepper
  2 large tomatoes, peeled, seeded,
     and chopped
  1 medium green pepper, finely
     chopped
  1 small yellow onion, finely
     chopped
  ¼ cup fresh lime juice
     Radish slices
     Ripe olives

1. Place fish in a shallow glass bowl; pour lemon juice over it. Refrigerate covered 6 hours, stirring occasionally. Drain; discard lemon juice.
2. Mix remaining ingredients except radish slices and olives with fish in a medium bowl. Refrigerate 30 minutes.
3. Serve on chilled plates; garnish with radish slices and olives. Or spoon into **fluted lemon shells.**

*8 servings (½ cup each)*

# Chilled Artichoke Plate

*Elegant in flavor and appearance. Serve with Individual Chicken Terrines (page 29) or Broiled Fish Quenelles (page 30) for an exquisite luncheon.*

  4 medium artichokes
     Chicken Stock (page 25)
  ¼ cup lemon juice
  1 teaspoon salt
  ½ pint cherry tomatoes
  ¾ cup Mock Béarnaise Sauce (page
     22)
*1 pound fresh asparagus, cut in
     2-inch pieces

1. Snip tips from artichoke leaves with scissors. Simmer artichokes in 1 inch of the stock with lemon juice and salt in a large covered saucepan until tender (about 45 minutes). Lift from pan with tongs; let cool. Refrigerate until chilled.
2. Carefully scoop seeds from tomatoes, using small end of a melon-ball cutter. Fill tomatoes with ¼ cup of the sauce; refrigerate.
3. Scrape choke from artichoke bottoms. Place artichokes in center of individual plates and dollop each with 2 tablespoons sauce. Arrange raw asparagus pieces and tomatoes attractively on plates. Serve immediately.

*4 servings*

*The flavor and texture of raw young asparagus is delightful. If asparagus is tough, simmer in 1 inch of stock until just tender (about 8 minutes); drain and refrigerate until chilled.
   Frozen asparagus (10 ounces) can be used; cook according to package directions and refrigerate until chilled.

## Celery Appetizer

*This lovely first course can be expanded to a luncheon entrée with the addition of shrimp or chicken.*

8 stalks celery, cut in julienne
    strips (about 3 cups)
½ cup Mock Mayonnaise (page
    22)
½ teaspoon celery seed, crushed
¼ teaspoon salt
2 teaspoons minced shallots
½ teaspoon wine vinegar
    Lettuce cups
    Pimento strips

Mix all ingredients, except lettuce and pimento, just until combined. Refrigerate covered until cold. Serve in lettuce cups; garnish with pimento.

*6 servings*

*Note:* If desired, mix in 1 cup cooked diced shrimp or chicken breast, increasing Mock Mayonnaise by 2 tablespoons. Season to taste with salt.

## Lombardy Green Tart

1 package (10 ounces) frozen
    chopped spinach, thawed
2 cups low-fat cottage cheese
1 medium zucchini, minced
2 stalks celery, minced
1 bunch green onions, green part
    only, minced
2 tablespoons snipped parsley
2 teaspoons snipped fresh or 1
    teaspoon dried marjoram
    leaves
2 teaspoons snipped fresh or 1
    teaspoon dried thyme leaves
4 eggs, lightly beaten
½ teaspoon salt
⅛ teaspoon freshly ground
    pepper
    Lettuce leaves

1. Press all liquid from spinach.
2. Combine all ingredients, except lettuce leaves, in a bowl. Mix thoroughly. Spoon mixture into a lightly oiled 9-inch pie plate.
3. Bake at 375°F 45 minutes. Cut into wedges to serve. Serve hot, or refrigerate until chilled and serve on lettuce.

*6 servings*

**Lombardy Green Salad:** Follow recipe for Lombardy Green Tart. Omit eggs, baking, and lettuce. Serve chilled on a bed of **fresh spinach leaves.**

## Vegetable Mélange with Mustard Sauce

1 large yellow squash or
    zucchini, pared and minced
3 medium carrots, minced
¼ cup minced onion
¼ cup minced dill pickle
4 ounces Swiss cheese, minced
⅓ cup prepared mustard
⅓ cup dill pickle juice
1 teaspoon sugar
½ teaspoon curry powder
1 garlic clove, minced
    Lettuce cups

Combine squash, carrot, onion, pickle, and cheese in a medium bowl. Mix remaining ingredients, except lettuce cups; pour over vegetables and stir to coat well. Refrigerate until well chilled. Serve in lettuce cups.

*6 servings*

Cold Roast Beef Vinaigrette, 40; Ham
Steak with Parsley Sauce, 45; Rack of Veal
with Peppercorn Sauce, 45.

# Pears with Roquefort

*This recipe can be served appropriately as a dessert as well as a first course.*

4 small pears
2 tablespoons Roquefort or blue cheese, crumbled
½ cup low-fat cottage cheese
¼ cup Neufchatel cheese
2 teaspoons brandy
2 tablespoons water
Watercress

1. Cut entire top off pears; reserve. Using melon-ball cutter, carefully scoop out pears, leaving a ¼-inch shell. Discard core and seeds. Finely chop pulp.
2. Purée pulp with cheeses, brandy, and water in a food processor or blender. Fill cavity of pears with cheese mixture. Replace tops on pears. Garnish with watercress. Serve with a knife and fork.

*4 servings*

# Savory Cheese Custards

1 large yellow onion
¼ teaspoon salt
1½ teaspoons poppy seed
1 cup instant nonfat dry-milk solids
2 cups water
2 teaspoons Worcestershire sauce
2 teaspoons Dijon mustard
¼ teaspoon salt
2 eggs
2 ounces Jarlsberg or Parmesan cheese, finely shredded

1. Bake onion at 400°F until tender when pierced with a fork (about 1½ hours). Let cool. Peel onion and chop finely (about 1½ cups). Mix onion with ¼ teaspoon salt and the poppy seed; spoon mixture into the bottom of 4 ramekins or custard cups.
2. Process dry-milk solids, water, Worcestershire sauce, mustard, ¼ teaspoon salt, and eggs in a food processor or blender until very smooth.
3. Pour mixture into ramekins; sprinkle cheese over mixture. Place ramekins in a shallow baking pan; pour 1 inch boiling water into pan.
4. Bake at 325°F 30 to 40 minutes, or until custard is set and a knife inserted between center and edge comes out clean. Serve warm, or refrigerate and serve cold.

*4 servings*

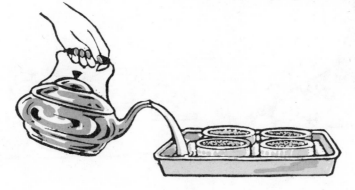

# Eggs Poached in Hot Sauce

*This recipe is similar to the traditional eggs ranchero from Mexico.*

2 cups Savory Tomato Sauce (page 23)
8 drops Tabasco or ¼ teaspoon chili powder
4 eggs
1 tablespoon snipped fresh coriander or parsley

1. Mix tomato sauce and Tabasco in a medium skillet; heat to simmering. Slip eggs into tomato sauce; cook covered over low heat until eggs are set (about 4 minutes).
2. Serve eggs with sauce in small shallow bowls or on small plates with rims; sprinkle with coriander.

*4 servings*

Fish Stew, 53;
Sole with Shrimp Pâté in Champagne, 50

## Jellied Consommé

2 envelopes unflavored gelatin
½ cup cold water
5 cups Beef Stock (page 25)
1 teaspoon Worcestershire sauce
1 tablespoon dry sherry
2 teaspoons lemon juice
Lemon twists
2 tablespoons chopped ripe
olives

1. Pour gelatin over cold water in a medium saucepan; let stand 5 minutes. Set over low heat until gelatin is dissolved (about 3 minutes), stirring occasionally. Stir in remaining ingredients, except lemon twists and olives. Heat thoroughly, then cool slightly.
2. Pour consommé into a mixing bowl; refrigerate covered until set (3 to 4 hours).
3. Beat slightly before serving. Spoon into consommé cups or wine glasses. Garnish with lemon twists and chopped olives.

*6 servings (about ¾ cup each)*

## Fragrant Mushroom Soup

*The flavor of the dried mushrooms is "woodsy" and full-bodied. The combination of fresh and dried mushrooms is unusual.*

1½ quarts Chicken Stock (page 25)
1 cup dried mushrooms
1 small onion, chopped
Salt
Freshly ground pepper
10 fresh mushrooms, cleaned and
sliced
Low-Fat Yogurt (page 19), if
desired

1. Pour 2 cups of the stock over the dried mushrooms in a bowl. Cover with a plate to keep mushrooms submerged. Let stand until mushrooms are soft (about 45 minutes). Drain; reserve liquid. Remove tough center stems with a sharp knife and discard; chop mushrooms.
2. Combine reserved mushroom liquid, remaining chicken stock, dried mushrooms, and onion in a medium saucepan. Simmer covered 30 minutes. Season to taste with salt and pepper. Stir fresh mushrooms into stock; cook 1 minute.
3. Serve immediately in soup cups. Top with dollops of yogurt, if desired.

*8 servings (¾ cup each)*

## Egg-Drop Soup

*The addition of rice and chicken livers adds heartiness to this Oriental favorite.*

6 cups Chicken Stock (page 25)
2 teaspoons clarified butter
¼ cup uncooked long-grain rice
6 chicken livers, cooked and
chopped
1 egg yolk, beaten
2 tablespoons snipped parsley
Salt
Freshly ground white pepper
1 tablespoon snipped chives

1. Heat stock to boiling in a medium saucepan.
2. Heat butter in a small skillet until bubbly; stir in rice. Cook and stir rice until lightly browned; stir into boiling stock. Simmer covered until rice is tender (about 25 minutes).
3. Stir liver, egg yolk, and parsley into stock; cook and stir until egg is cooked and liver hot (about 2 minutes). Season to taste with salt and pepper.
4. Spoon into bowls; garnish with chives.

*6 servings (1⅓ cups each)*

## Spinach Soup with Onion Petals

8 small onions, peeled
6 cups Chicken Stock (page 25)
2 pounds fresh spinach, washed and stems removed
3 cups water
Salt
1 tablespoon finely chopped green onion tops

1. Cut each onion into ¼-inch slices, cutting almost to, but not through, base. Give onion a quarter turn; cut into ¼-inch slices, intersecting previous slices.
2. Simmer onions in stock in a large covered skillet or saucepan until onions are tender (about 20 minutes).
3. Simmer spinach in water in a covered saucepan 10 minutes; drain, adding cooking liquid to stock with onions. Reserve spinach for other use.
4. Taste stock; add salt if necessary. Lift onions from stock and into individual soup bowls with slotted spoon. Ladle stock around onions in each bowl. Sprinkle with green onion tops. Serve with knives, forks, and spoons.

*8 servings (1 cup each)*

## Jellied Gazpacho

*Colorful Mexican fare that is a traditional crowd pleaser.*

4 cups chilled tomato juice
2 envelopes unflavored gelatin
1 cup Low-Fat Yogurt (page 19)
1 garlic clove, minced
1 pound tomatoes, peeled, seeded, and chopped
1 small cucumber, pared, seeded, and chopped
1 medium green pepper, chopped
⅓ cup shredded carrot
2 tablespoons minced red onion
½ cup finely chopped celery
3 tablespoons fresh lemon juice
1 to 1½ teaspoons salt
¼ teaspoon freshly ground pepper
⅛ teaspoon chili powder
2 garlic cloves, minced
Salad greens

1. Pour ½ cup of the tomato juice into a small saucepan. Sprinkle the gelatin over the juice; let stand 5 minutes. Set over low heat, stirring constantly, until gelatin is dissolved (about 3 minutes).
2. Pour mixture and remaining tomato juice into a large mixing bowl. Refrigerate until slightly thickened, but not set.
3. Mix yogurt and garlic; refrigerate covered.
4. Stir vegetables, lemon juice, salt, pepper, chili powder, and 2 garlic cloves into tomato mixture. Mix well.
5. Spoon tomato mixture into 6 individual soup bowls or a 2-quart bowl. Refrigerate covered until mixture has set (about 4 hours).
6. Unmold on salad greens and serve with the garlic yogurt.

*6 servings (about 1 cup each)*

*Note:* Jellied Gazpacho is excellent for lunch served with steamed shrimp.

## Yogurt Soup

*Middle Eastern influence has been translated for this rich, filling, but low-calorie soup.*

1½ quarts Chicken Stock (page 25)
2 tablespoons cornstarch
1 cup Low-Fat Yogurt (page 19)
Juice of ½ lemon, if desired
2 teaspoons clarified butter
¼ teaspoon paprika
Snipped parsley

1. Heat stock to boiling. Mix cornstarch thoroughly with yogurt; stir into stock. Simmer, stirring rapidly, until stock mixture thickens slightly (about 4 minutes). Taste; add lemon juice if needed for tartness.
2. Melt butter; stir in paprika. Spoon butter mixture onto top of soup. Pour soup into bowls. Sprinkle with parsley.

*8 servings (¾ cup each)*

# Chicken-Mushroom Pudding

*Though soufflélike in texture, this recipe has only half the eggs, flour, and butter of a soufflé.*

1 tablespoon butter
1 tablespoon flour
½ cup nonfat dry-milk solids
½ cup cold water
½ cup Chicken Stock (page 25)
1¼ cups finely chopped cooked
    chicken
1 cup finely chopped mushrooms
2 teaspoons snipped parsley
1 tablespoon finely snipped
    chives or green onion tops
2 teaspoons Dijon mustard
½ teaspoon salt
¼ teaspoon freshly ground
    pepper
2 egg yolks
3 egg whites
    Shredded carrot or radish roses

1. Melt butter in a medium skillet; mix in flour, stirring constantly until mixture is smooth and bubbly. Remove from heat. Mix milk solids, water, and stock; stir into flour mixture gradually. Return sauce to heat; boil and stir until thickened (about 2 minutes). Stir in remaining ingredients, except eggs and carrot. Cook and stir 3 minutes; let cool to room temperature.
2. Beat egg yolks; stir into chicken mixture. Beat egg whites until stiff but not dry peaks form; fold gently into chicken mixture until blended. Spoon mixture into lightly buttered 1-quart soufflé dish.
3. Bake at 350°F 35 to 40 minutes, or until puffy and light brown. Garnish with carrot. Serve immediately.

*6 to 8 servings*

*Note:* Chicken-Mushroom Pudding is also delicious served cold. Let cool 30 minutes after baking, then refrigerate covered until completely chilled (about 4 hours).

# Spiced Pumpkin Soup

*The crunchy green pepper garnish adds an interesting texture and flavor contrast to this soup.*

1 small pumpkin (about 3
    pounds), pared and cut in
    2-inch pieces; or 2½ cups
    canned pumpkin
1 cup chopped onion
1 teaspoon minced ginger root
3 cups Chicken Stock (page 25)
½ teaspoon salt
½ teaspoon freshly ground
    pepper
½ teaspoon ground cloves
½ cup white wine
1¼ cups chopped green pepper

1. Simmer pumpkin, onion, and ginger root in stock in a covered saucepan until pumpkin is tender (about 20 minutes).
2. Purée mixture in two batches in a food processor or blender. Pour purée back into saucepan; stir in remaining ingredients except green pepper. Simmer uncovered 10 minutes.
3. Serve soup in bowls; garnish with green pepper.

*6 servings (about ¾ cup each)*

*Note:* This soup is also excellent served cold. If desired, Low-Fat Yogurt (page 19) can be used in place of the wine, or as a garnish.

# MEAT

Meat dishes in New French Cooking are in a sense far more wide ranging than in classic cooking. Although classic dishes could be varied by the hundreds of sauces in the chef's repertory, a fairly limited number of meat cuts were used—primarily the elegant beef roasts, tournedos or filet mignon steaks, legs and racks of lamb, veal roasts and medallions, and some organ meats.

The new cookery not only abandons the rich classic sauces, but it branches out to use many more meat cuts and styles of preparation. In this book the meat cuts include beef chuck roast, sirloin steak, ground beef, skirt steak, rib roast, pork chops, ham steak, lamb cubes, leg of lamb, veal scallops, veal breast, and liver.

Influences from foreign countries are also felt and adapted with a French approach. French peasant cooking is given attention and reworked with some refinements.

Most of the meat recipes in this chapter have their own light sauces. You could also design additional New French meat dishes by adding sauces (see pages 18–26) to roasts, chops, and steaks.

Classic French cookery does not consider pork a proper meat for fine dining, and it is given only slight attention by the new-style chefs in France. French pork still may be overly fatty, not like the modern lean pork in the United States. In this book pork is used, as it is no higher in calories than other meats.

## Herbed Skirt Steak

*Mock Crème Fraîche and fresh dill enhance this creative combination.*

- 1½ pounds lean beef skirt steak
- 2 teaspoons clarified butter
- 1 large yellow onion, finely sliced
- ½ cup Beef Stock (page 25)
- 1 garlic clove, minced
- ¼ teaspoon freshly ground pepper
- 1½ teaspoons salt
- ½ cup Mock Crème Fraîche (page 18)
- ¼ cup snipped fresh dill or 2 tablespoons dried dill weed

1. Slice steak in half lengthwise; cut pieces across the grain into paper-thin slices. Heat butter over high heat in a 12-inch skillet. Add meat slices, stirring quickly to coat meat with butter. Add onion; cook and stir 2 minutes. Add Beef Stock, garlic, pepper, and salt; simmer covered until onion is tender (about 3 minutes).

2. Stir ¼ cup pan juices into Mock Crème Fraîche. Stir mixture back into pan; stir in dill. Serve immediately.

*4 to 6 servings*

## Steak with Mushroom Stuffing

*The texture of fresh mushrooms and the flavor of nutmeg are memorable additions to a perfectly cooked steak.*

- 1 small onion, finely chopped
- 2 shallots, finely chopped
- 2 tablespoons Beef Stock (page 25)
- ½ pound mushrooms, cleaned and chopped
- 1 tablespoon brandy
- 3 grinds fresh or ¼ teaspoon ground nutmeg
- ¾ teaspoon salt
- ¼ teaspoon freshly ground pepper
- 2½ pounds lean beef sirloin steak, boneless
- Snipped parsley

1. Simmer onion and shallots in stock until tender (about 5 minutes). Mix onion, shallots, mushrooms, brandy, nutmeg, salt, and pepper.

2. Trim excess fat from steak. Cut pocket in steak, cutting to, but not through opposite side and leaving 1 inch intact on each end. Fill pocket loosely with onion mixture; skewer opening with wooden picks.

3. Broil steak 3 inches from heat, 8 minutes on each side for medium rare, 10 minutes on each side for medium. Remove wooden picks. Sprinkle steak with parsley. Slice and serve.

*8 servings*

# Pot Roast Jardinière

*A country-style stew with garden vegetables is hearty fare.*

1 beef chuck pot roast (4 pounds)
¼ cup prepared horseradish
1 tablespoon salt
1 medium tomato, chopped
1 cup Beef Stock (page 25)
3 medium kohlrabi or turnips, pared and cut in ½-inch cubes
3 medium carrots, cut in ½-inch slices
*1 pound fresh Brussels sprouts, cleaned
1 teaspoon snipped fresh or ½ teaspoon dried thyme leaves
1 teaspoon snipped fresh or ½ teaspoon dried marjoram leaves
1 teaspoon salt
½ teaspoon pepper
2 leeks, cut in 1-inch pieces
2 teaspoons arrowroot
Cold water

1. Rub meat on both sides with a mixture of horseradish and 1 tablespoon salt; place meat in a Dutch oven. Add tomato and stock to Dutch oven. Cover.
2. Cook in a 325°F oven about 3 hours, or until meat is tender.
3. Add vegetables, thyme, marjoram, 1 teaspoon salt, and ½ teaspoon pepper to Dutch oven during last 15 minutes of cooking time; cook just until vegetables are tender.
4. Remove meat and vegetables to platter. Skim fat from cooking liquid. If thicker sauce is desired, mix arrowroot with a little cold water and stir into liquid. Simmer, stirring constantly, until sauce is thickened. Pass sauce.

*6 servings*

*1 package (10 ounces) frozen Brussels sprouts can be substituted for the fresh. Add to Dutch oven for length of cooking time indicated on package.

# Oriental One-Pot Meal

*This recipe has been borrowed from Japanese sukiyaki. The technique is perfect for New French Cooking, as foods are cooked quickly in stock to retain natural color, flavor, and texture.*

6 cups Beef Stock (page 25)
¼ cup light soy sauce
⅓ cup beer
2 teaspoons sugar
*¼ teaspoon freshly ground Szechuan or black pepper
½ teaspoon salt
2 cups sliced fresh mushrooms
2 bunches green onions, cut in ½-inch pieces
1 cup sliced bamboo shoots
**1 cup sliced Chinese cabbage or bok choy
1½ pounds lean beef sirloin or rib eye steak, cut in paper-thin slices

1. Mix stock, soy sauce, beer, sugar, pepper, and salt in a 3-quart saucepan. Boil 3 minutes. Simmer vegetables in stock mixture until vegetables are just tender (about 5 minutes). Divide vegetables among 6 shallow bowls; keep warm in oven.
2. Cook half the beef slices in the simmering stock mixture until rare to medium done (2 to 4 minutes). Divide meat among bowls. Cook remaining meat; divide among bowls. Serve hot stock mixture over meat and vegetables or in individual bowls for dipping.

*6 servings*

*Lightly roast Szechuan pepper over medium heat in a skillet before grinding.
**Chinese cabbage can be purchased in Oriental or specialty shops.

# Cold Roast Beef Vinaigrette

*Use freshly cooked or leftover beef for this superb entrée. Stock replaces oil in the marinade. Your own selection of vegetables can be used for color and texture contrast.*

1½ pounds cooked medium-rare roast beef, sliced ¼ inch thick and cut in 2-inch-wide strips
3 stalks celery, cut in ¼-inch pieces
1 medium tomato, chopped
2 sweet red or green peppers, chopped in ¼-inch pieces
1 tablespoon finely chopped red onion
1 tablespoon olive oil
2 tablespoons wine vinegar
¼ cup Beef Stock (page 25)
2 teaspoons snipped fresh or 1 teaspoon dried basil leaves
1 teaspoon snipped fresh or ½ teaspoon dried coriander leaves (cilantro)
1 tablespoon snipped parsley
1 teaspoon salt
*¼ teaspoon freshly ground Szechuan or black pepper
1 teaspoon snipped fresh or ½ teaspoon dried oregano leaves
2 garlic cloves, finely minced
2 teaspoons Dijon mustard

1. Arrange beef in a shallow glass dish. Mix remaining ingredients and pour over meat. Refrigerate covered 8 hours or overnight.
2. Taste meat and marinade; adjust seasoning, if desired. Let stand at room temperature 45 minutes before serving. Serve beef slices topped with marinade.

*4 to 6 servings*

*Lightly roast Szechuan pepper over medium heat in a skillet before grinding.

# Beef-on-Tomato Medallions

*Oriental stir-frying is a perfect technique for use in New French Cooking as little oil is used and the foods are cooked quickly to retain natural color, flavor, and texture.*

3 large ripe tomatoes
Salt
Freshly ground pepper
1 tablespoon vegetable oil
½ teaspoon sesame or walnut oil
2½ pounds lean beef sirloin steak, boneless, cut in paper-thin slices
2 bunches green onions, cut in ¾-inch pieces
1 tablespoon light soy sauce
2 tablespoons dry white wine
¼ teaspoon sugar
½ teaspoon salt

1. Slice each tomato into 4 slices horizontally. Sprinkle with salt and pepper. Bake on a cookie sheet at 325°F until hot (about 15 minutes).
2. Heat vegetable and sesame oils in a wok or skillet until hot but not smoking. Add meat, stirring to coat pieces. Cook 1 minute. Add green onions. Cook and stir 1 minute. Mix soy sauce, wine, sugar, and ½ teaspoon salt; pour over meat. Cook and stir until meat is done (about 3 minutes).
3. Overlap 2 tomato slices at the side of each serving plate. Arrange meat mixture on plates, partially covering tomatoes.

*6 servings*

*Note:* Sesame and walnut oils can be purchased in specialty or gourmet shops. These oils have a delicate but distinct flavor which provides an interesting accent in this recipe. The oil can be omitted, or vegetable oil substituted.

# Meat-Stuffed Cabbage

*A whole cabbage encases a flavorful and moist meat-and-vegetable combination.*

1 large head cabbage (about 4
    pounds)
  Water
1 tablespoon salt
  Cheesecloth
2 pounds lean ground beef
2 bunches green onions, cut in
    ¼-inch pieces
1 garlic clove, minced
1 medium zucchini, finely
    chopped (reserve 8 thin slices
    for garnish)
1 large green pepper, chopped
1 egg, slightly beaten
1 cup fine soft bread crumbs
    made from whole-grain
    bread
1½ teaspoons snipped fresh or ¾
    teaspoon dried basil leaves
2 teaspoons snipped fresh or 1
    teaspoon dried thyme leaves
2 teaspoons snipped fresh or 1
    teaspoon dried rosemary
    leaves
2 teaspoons salt
½ teaspoon freshly ground
    pepper
1 can (16 ounces) plum tomatoes
    (reserve liquid)
4 fresh mushrooms, cut in half,
    for garnish
  Water

1. Place cabbage in a Dutch oven. Cover with boiling water; add 1 tablespoon salt. Simmer covered until outer leaves are softened but still firm (about 10 minutes). Drain cabbage; rinse with cold water. Have cheesecloth ready for wrapping stuffed cabbage.

2. Mix remaining ingredients, except the reserved zucchini slices and the mushrooms, until well blended.

3. Core cabbage and pull outside leaves back. Remove inside of cabbage carefully, leaving outside layer 5 or 6 leaves thick. Lay outer leaves on a double thickness of cheesecloth; fill leaves with meat mixture. Wrap stuffed cabbage tightly in cheesecloth; invert on another piece of cheesecloth so that the opening of the cabbage is on the bottom. Wrap cabbage securely, tying the cheesecloth into a handle at the top. Lift wrapped cabbage into Dutch oven. Pour reserved tomato liquid around cabbage. Cover.

4. Bake at 350°F to an internal temperature of 165°F (about 1½ hours). Check temperature by inserting a meat thermometer through leaves and into center of meat. Lift cabbage out of Dutch oven; let stand 10 minutes.

5. While cabbage is standing, place zucchini slices and mushrooms in a medium saucepan. Simmer in a small amount of water until barely tender (about 3 minutes); drain.

6. Remove outside layer of cheesecloth from cabbage; place a pie plate on cabbage and invert. Remove remaining cheesecloth; place serving platter on cabbage and invert. Gently shape cabbage with hands if necessary. Garnish top of cabbage with zucchini slices and mushrooms. Cut into wedges and serve.

*8 to 10 servings*

# Hearty Beef-Cabbage Soup

2 cups tomato juice
4 cups Beef Stock (page 25)
2 cups shredded red cabbage
1 medium onion, thinly sliced
1 carrot, thinly sliced
3 cups cooked beef cubes
2 tablespoons dark raisins
1 teaspoon caraway seed
1 teaspoon paprika
1 teaspoon salt
1 tablespoon cider vinegar
  Low-Fat Yogurt (page 19), if
    desired, for garnish

Simmer all ingredients in a Dutch oven 20 minutes, stirring occasionally. Serve in bowls. Garnish with dollops of yogurt.

*6 servings (2 cups each)*

*Note:* This recipe can be made without the meat and served as a first course.

# Steak Tartare with Vegetables

2 pounds beef sirloin steak, boneless
⅓ cup finely chopped leek or green onion
1½ teaspoons Worcestershire sauce
¼ teaspoon Tabasco
1 teaspoon Dijon mustard
½ teaspoon salt
Freshly ground Szechuan or black pepper
1 egg yolk, if desired
1 teaspoon drained capers
2 bunches parsley, stems removed
1 green pepper, cut in 1-inch pieces
1 sweet red pepper, cut in 1-inch pieces
1 large zucchini, cut in ¼-inch slices
1 medium cucumber, cut in ¼-inch slices
12 medium mushrooms, cut in half lengthwise
1 large carrot, cut in ¼-inch slices
12 large red or white radishes, cut in half

1. Chop meat coarsely in a food processor (or have butcher grind meat coarsely 2 times). Place beef, leek, Worcestershire sauce, Tabasco, mustard, salt, and pepper in a mixing bowl; mix quickly and lightly with 2 forks. Taste; adjust seasonings.
2. Mound beef on a medium serving platter. Make an indentation in top of mound; slip egg yolk into indentation. Sprinkle beef with capers. Surround beef with a thick rim of parsley. Arrange vegetables on parsley. Serve immediately with knives for spreading beef mixture on vegetables.

*8 servings*

*Note:* For a party, this recipe would make about 48 appetizer servings.

# Elegant Leg of Lamb

*A coating of Dijon mustard, spices, coffee, and wine lends pleasing flavor to the lamb.*

1 lamb leg, whole (about 6 pounds)
2 garlic cloves, each sliced in 3 pieces
1 tablespoon Dijon mustard
1 tablespoon strong coffee
2 teaspoons ground ginger
1 cup strong black coffee
¼ cup white port wine
1 cup Chicken Stock (page 25)
4 teaspoons arrowroot
Cold water
2 teaspoons butter, if desired

1. Trim excess fat from roast. Cut 6 small slits in the roast and insert garlic slices. Rub mixture of mustard, 1 tablespoon coffee, and ginger over entire surface of roast.
2. Place in a shallow roasting pan. Insert meat thermometer so that tip is in center of meat, away from bone and fat.
3. Roast in a 325°F oven to an internal temperature of 175°F (about 3 hours). Mix 1 cup coffee and wine; baste roast with mixture several times during last hour of roasting time.
4. Remove roast to meat platter. Cover loosely with a tent of aluminum foil.
5. Carefully spoon fat from roasting pan. Add remaining basting mixture and stock to roasting pan. Heat to boiling, stirring to incorporate meat particles from pan. Mix arrowroot with a little cold water. Stir into stock mixture. Simmer, stirring constantly, until mixture thickens. Stir butter into gravy just before serving.

*6 to 8 servings*

# Fruited Lamb Roast

*A boned leg of lamb is filled with marinated dried fruits and roasted. The fruit is then puréed for an elegant sauce.*

½ pound dried pears or apples
½ pound dried apricots
½ cup golden raisins
1 teaspoon finely minced ginger root or ½ teaspoon ground ginger
1 tablespoon grated orange peel
Juice of 1 orange
½ cup bourbon
Apple cider (about 3 cups)
1 lamb leg, boneless (about 4 pounds)
½ cup bourbon
Apple cider
Salt
2 tablespoons bourbon
Apple cider

1. Place pears, apricots, raisins, ginger root, orange peel, orange juice, and ½ cup bourbon in a medium saucepan. Pour in enough apple cider to cover fruits. Simmer uncovered 20 minutes; cool.

2. Trim roast of excess fat. Lay roast flat in a shallow glass casserole. Drain fruit. Add ½ cup bourbon to drained juice; add enough apple cider to measure 2 cups. Pour juice mixture over roast. Refrigerate roast covered 8 hours or overnight. Refrigerate fruits covered.

3. Remove roast from marinade; salt lightly on both sides. Arrange one third of the fruit on surface of meat; roll up and tie with string at intervals.

4. Place roast on rack in a roasting pan. Insert meat thermometer so tip is in center of roast.

5. Roast uncovered in a 325°F oven to an internal temperature of 175°F (about 2 hours). Add remaining fruit to roasting pan during last half hour of cooking.

6. Place roast and half the fruit on a serving platter. Cover lightly with aluminum foil. Let stand 20 minutes before carving.

7. Purée remaining fruit in a blender or food processor with 2 tablespoons bourbon and enough apple cider to make a sauce consistency. Heat thoroughly; serve with the roast.

*8 to 10 servings*

# Lamb and Pork in Cognac

*The flavors of these two meats blend uniquely while cooking. Choose your favorite fresh vegetable to add to this recipe.*

⅓ cup cognac
1⅔ cups dry white wine
½ teaspoon ground mace
¼ teaspoon ground cinnamon
½ teaspoon salt
1½ pounds lean lamb stew cubes
1½ pounds lean pork stew cubes
3 stalks celery, finely chopped
3 carrots, finely chopped
1 medium yellow onion, finely chopped
2 teaspoons salt
½ pound baby carrots
½ pound fresh broccoli
½ pound baby white onions
Chicken Stock (page 25)
Salt
Freshly ground pepper

1. Mix cognac, wine, mace, cinnamon, and ½ teaspoon salt; pour over meat cubes in a shallow glass bowl. Refrigerate covered 6 hours or overnight; stir occasionally. Drain meat, reserving ¾ cup marinade.

2. Mix chopped vegetables and layer them in bottom of a Dutch oven; pour reserved marinade over and simmer on top of range 5 minutes. Layer meat cubes over vegetables and sprinkle with 2 teaspoons salt. Cover Dutch oven.

3. Bake at 350°F 1½ to 2 hours, or until meat is tender.

4. Simmer vegetables in 1 inch of stock until just tender (about 15 minutes). Season with salt and pepper.

5. Remove meat from Dutch oven with a slotted spoon to a shallow serving dish; arrange attractively with vegetables.

*6 servings*

# Lamb Ratatouille

*In this main-dish version of ratatouille, the vegetables remain crisp and flavorful.*

1 quart Savory Tomato Sauce
(page 23)
1 tablespoon snipped fresh or
1½ teaspoons dried coriander
leaves
2 pounds lean lamb stew cubes
2 teaspoons salt
Freshly ground pepper
2 tablespoons fresh lemon juice
¼ cup dry vermouth or dry white
wine
1 small eggplant, pared and cut
in 1-inch cubes
Salted water
2 green peppers, cut in 1-inch
squares
2 medium zucchini, cut in
½-inch slices
2 medium yellow onions, cut in
¼-inch slices
Chicken Stock (page 25)
Salt
Freshly ground pepper
1 tablespoon olive oil
Snipped coriander

1. Spoon tomato sauce into bottom of a Dutch oven; sprinkle with 1 tablespoon coriander. Place lamb cubes in sauce; sprinkle with 2 teaspoons salt, pepper, and lemon juice. Pour vermouth over meat. Simmer covered until lamb is tender (about 2 hours).
2. Soak eggplant in salted water to cover for 1 hour; drain and pat dry.
3. Cook vegetables during last half hour lamb is cooking. Simmer eggplant, green peppers, zucchini, and onions in ½ inch of stock in a large skillet until barely tender, so vegetables retain their shape and texture.
4. Arrange cooked vegetables attractively on a heatproof platter; keep warm in oven. Season vegetables with salt and pepper; drizzle with olive oil. Arrange lamb and tomato mixture over vegetables; sprinkle with coriander.

*6 servings*

# Pork Chops Piquant

*Green pepper and onion stay crisp in this braised pork chop dish. Capers add a hint of pungency.*

4 pork loin chops, 1 inch thick
¼ cup water
¼ teaspoon bottled brown
bouquet sauce
½ teaspoon salt
Freshly ground pepper
½ cup Chicken Stock (page 25)
¼ cup dry white wine
1 green pepper, chopped
1 medium yellow onion, chopped
2 tablespoons capers, drained
Watercress or parsley sprigs

1. Trim excess fat from chops. Brush chops lightly with a mixture of water and brown bouquet sauce. Brown chops lightly on both sides in a nonstick skillet over medium heat. Sprinkle with salt and pepper.
2. Add stock and wine. Simmer covered 30 minutes. Skim fat from liquid. Stir in green pepper, onion, and capers. Simmer uncovered 10 to 15 minutes until vegetables are just tender. Taste vegetables and sauce; adjust seasoning.
3. Serve vegetables and sauce over chops; garnish with watercress.

*4 servings*

# Ham Steak with Parsley Sauce

2 bunches parsley, washed and
    stems removed
¼ cup dry white wine
1 center-cut smoked ham steak,
    ¾ inch thick (about 1½
    pounds)
⅔ cup Mock Hollandaise Sauce
    (page 22)
    Salt
    Freshly ground white pepper

1. Line bottom of a shallow baking dish with half the parsley; drizzle with half the wine. Lay ham steak on parsley. Cover ham with remaining parsley; drizzle with remaining wine. Lightly cover baking dish.
2. Bake at 325°F about 30 minutes, or until ham is thoroughly heated.
3. Make Mock Hollandaise Sauce while ham is baking; keep warm.
4. Place ham on platter; cover lightly with aluminum foil. Purée cooked parsley in a blender or food processor; stir mixture into Mock Hollandaise Sauce. Season sauce with salt and pepper. Heat sauce thoroughly; serve with ham.

*3 or 4 servings*

# Ham Mousse on Medallions

6 slices boiled ham, cut ⅓ inch
    thick (about 1½ pounds)
2 teaspoons unflavored gelatin
1 cup cold water
2 cups low-fat ricotta cheese
3 tablespoons snipped parsley
1½ tablespoons snipped fresh or 2
    teaspoons crumbled dried
    tarragon leaves
2 teaspoons Dijon mustard
⅛ teaspoon salt
    Dash freshly ground pepper
    Parsley sprigs
    Radish roses

1. Cut two 2½-inch circles from each slice ham; refrigerate covered. Mince remaining ham pieces; refrigerate covered.
2. Sprinkle gelatin over cold water in a saucepan; let stand 5 minutes. Set over low heat until dissolved (about 3 minutes), stirring occasionally.
3. Pour gelatin into a food processor or blender; add ricotta cheese, snipped parsley, tarragon, mustard, salt, and pepper. Process until mixture is smooth; transfer mixture to a medium mixing bowl. Stir in minced ham; refrigerate covered until mixture has set (about 1 hour).
4. Place 2 ham circles on each of 6 individual plates. Mound mousse by heaping tablespoonfuls on circles. Garnish with parsley and radish roses.

*6 servings*

*Note:* This recipe will make 12 first-course servings.

# Rack of Veal with Peppercorn Sauce

*Very easy to prepare, very elegant to serve. Green peppercorns add zest to a low-calorie version of Béarnaise Sauce.*

1 veal rib roast (about 5 pounds)
1 teaspoon salt
    Freshly ground white pepper
    White wine
1⅓ cups Mock Béarnaise Sauce
    (page 22; double recipe)
2 tablespoons drained green
    peppercorns

1. Rub roast with salt and pepper; place in a roasting pan. Insert meat thermometer so tip is in center of meat, away from bone.
2. Roast uncovered in a 325°F oven to an internal temperature of 165°F (about 3 hours). Baste several times with white wine during last hour of roasting. Remove to a platter and cover loosely with aluminum foil; let stand 20 minutes before carving.
3. While roast is standing, make the sauce, adding peppercorns before heating. Pass sauce.

*10 servings*

*Note:* A boneless veal roast can also be used in this recipe. Roast as directed above, allowing about 35 minutes per pound.

# Savory Veal Stew

*The meat in this stew is unbelievably tender. Caraway and fennel provide a flavorful accent to garden vegetables.*

- 3 pounds veal stew cubes
- 1½ teaspoons salt
- ½ teaspoon freshly ground pepper
- 2 garlic cloves
- 1 teaspoon caraway seed, lightly crushed
- 1 teaspoon fennel seed, lightly crushed
- 2 bay leaves
- ½ cup dry white wine
- 1 cup Beef Stock (page 25)
- 1 small head cabbage, cut in 8 wedges
- 3 leeks, cut in 3-inch pieces
- ¾ teaspoon salt
- ½ teaspoon freshly ground pepper
- 1 tablespoon arrowroot
  Cold water
- ½ pound mushrooms, sliced
- ½ cup Mock Crème Fraîche (page 18), if desired

1. Place veal in a 6-quart Dutch oven; sprinkle with 1½ teaspoons salt and ½ teaspoon pepper. Mix garlic, caraway, fennel, bay leaves, wine, and stock. Pour over veal. Simmer covered over low heat 2 hours.
2. Add cabbage and leeks to Dutch oven; sprinkle with ¾ teaspoon salt and ½ teaspoon pepper. Simmer covered until vegetables and veal are just tender (about 15 minutes). Remove veal and vegetables to a shallow serving dish; keep warm.
3. Skim fat from cooking liquid in Dutch oven. Discard bay leaves. Mix arrowroot with a little cold water. Stir into cooking liquid; simmer until thickened (about 3 minutes). Stir in mushrooms and Mock Crème Fraîche; simmer 1 minute. Pour thickened mixture over veal and vegetables. Sprinkle with **parsley.**

*8 servings*

# Veal Scallops in Lemon Sauce

*This adaptation of Veal Piccata uses stock rather than butter in the sauce. Szechuan pepper adds a flavor accent to the tart sauce; fresh snipped parsley adds color.*

- 12 veal scallops (about 2 pounds)
- ¼ cup water
- ¼ teaspoon bottled brown bouquet sauce
- 2 teaspoons clarified butter
  Salt
- ¾ cup dry white wine
- ¾ cup Chicken Stock (page 25)
- ⅓ cup finely chopped onion
- 1 garlic clove, minced
- ½ cup fresh lemon juice
- ¼ teaspoon freshly ground white pepper
- ½ teaspoon salt
- 1 tablespoon arrowroot
  Cold water
- 1 tablespoon snipped parsley

1. Pound veal scallops with a mallet until thin and even in thickness. Brush both sides lightly with a mixture of water and brown bouquet sauce. Cook a few pieces of veal in hot butter in a skillet just until done (about 1 minute on each side). Sprinkle lightly with salt. Keep warm in oven while cooking remaining veal.
2. While veal is cooking, mix wine, stock, onion, and garlic in a small saucepan. Simmer until onion is tender (about 3 minutes). Stir in lemon juice, pepper, and salt.
3. Mix arrowroot with a little cold water. Stir into simmering stock mixture. Simmer, stirring constantly, until mixture thickens.
4. Arrange veal on warm plates. Pour sauce over. Sprinkle with parsley.

*6 servings*

# Stuffed Veal Breast

*Spinach and ricotta cheese are in the filling for this tempting dish with an Italian influence.*

2½ pounds boneless breast of veal
   Salt
   Freshly ground pepper
1 large onion, chopped
2 tablespoons Chicken Stock
   (page 25)
*½ pound fresh spinach, washed
   and stems removed
¾ cup low-fat ricotta cheese
¼ cup grated Jarlsberg or
   Parmesan cheese
2 garlic cloves, minced
1 teaspoon snipped fresh or ½
   teaspoon dried thyme leaves
1½ teaspoons snipped fresh or ¾
   teaspoon dried basil leaves
½ teaspoon snipped fresh or ¼
   teaspoon dried oregano
   leaves
2 tablespoons snipped parsley
1 teaspoon salt
¼ teaspoon pepper
½ cup dry white wine or Chicken
   Stock

1. Trim excess fat from meat. Sprinkle meat lightly on both sides with salt and pepper.
2. Simmer onion in stock just until tender (about 5 minutes).
3. Place spinach with water clinging to leaves in a large saucepan; cook covered over medium heat just until wilted (about 3 minutes).
4. Drain onion and spinach well in a strainer, pressing moisture out with a wooden spoon. Mix onion, spinach, cheeses, garlic, thyme, basil, oregano, parsley, 1 teaspoon salt, and ¼ teaspoon pepper. Spoon mixture on surface of meat; roll up and tie with string at intervals. Place meat in a roasting pan. Pour wine over roast. Cover.
5. Roast in a 325°F oven about 1½ hours, or until tender.
6. Remove roast to a serving platter. Cover lightly with aluminum foil. Let stand 15 minutes before carving.

*6 servings*

*1 package (10 ounces) frozen spinach can be substituted for the fresh. Thaw and drain thoroughly in strainer.

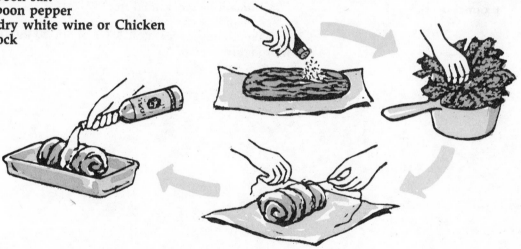

# Calf's Liver with Curried Onions

*The addition of curry and raisins gives this recipe an interesting Indian accent.*

1 large yellow onion, sliced
¼ cup sherry
½ teaspoon curry powder
½ teaspoon salt
   Freshly ground pepper
¼ cup golden raisins
2 teaspoons clarified butter
1 pound calf's liver
   Clarified butter

1. Simmer onion slices in wine in a medium skillet until onion is tender and wine is absorbed (about 10 minutes). Stir in curry powder, salt, pepper, raisins, and 2 teaspoons butter.
2. While onion is cooking, brush liver slices very lightly with clarified butter.
3. Broil 4 inches from heat until lightly browned (about 3 minutes on each side). Serve with onion.

*4 servings*

# Continental Veal Casserole

*Flavors of veal, ham, and cheese blend to make this an elegant company casserole.*

¾ pound fresh mushrooms, finely chopped
3 shallots, minced
⅓ cup dry white wine
Salt
¾ cup Chicken Stock (page 25)
⅔ cup Mock Crème Fraîche (page 18)
9 veal scallops (about 1½ pounds)
¼ cup water
¼ teaspoon bottled brown bouquet sauce
2 teaspoons clarified butter
Salt
6 thin slices cooked ham (about ⅓ pound)
1 can (15 ounces) artichoke bottoms, cut horizontally in 3 slices
12 thin slices Swiss cheese (about 6 ounces)

1. Mix mushrooms, shallots, and wine in a small skillet. Cook uncovered over low heat 5 minutes. Stir in salt to taste; set aside.

2. Heat stock in a small saucepan. Add a small amount of hot stock to Mock Crème Fraîche; stir mixture into stock; set aside.

3. Pound veal scallops with a mallet until thin and even in thickness. Brush both sides lightly with a mixture of water and brown bouquet sauce. Cook several pieces quickly in hot butter in a skillet until lightly browned (about 1 minute on each side). Salt veal lightly. Keep warm in oven while cooking remaining veal.

4. Layer ingredients in a large flat casserole in the following order:

  half the mushroom mixture
  half the veal scallops
  half the stock mixture
  the ham slices
  the artichoke bottoms
  half the cheese slices
  remaining veal scallops
  remaining mushroom mixture
  remaining stock mixture
  remaining cheese slices

5. Bake, lightly covered, at 350°F about 20 minutes, or until thoroughly heated.

*6 servings*

# FISH
# AND SHELLFISH

Adapting French recipes to the American kitchen is perhaps most difficult when it comes to fish and seafood. There are so many European varieties that simply are not available in this country. Thus, substitutions need to be made with fish that are similar in flavor, texture, and fat content.

A further problem is that fresh fish is difficult or impossible to find in many parts of the United States, especially in inland areas. Fish is flown to markets in large cities, but smaller communities must rely on frozen fish. Unfortunately, the quality of much frozen fish is substandard, especially for French cooking.

Nevertheless, try as best you can to get good fresh fish or only top-quality frozen fish. The recipes in this book call for both fresh-water and salt-water fish. In many cases other varieties can be substituted for those specified. Thus, if you can't get fresh whitefish or good sole, you might use frozen trout or fish caught in a local stream. Avoid the inexpensive varieties that come boxed in one-pound blocks.

## Citrus Steamed Salmon and Shrimp

1½ pounds salmon fillets, cut in 2x1-inch pieces
¾ pound uncooked shelled shrimp
½ cup lemon juice
¼ cup lime juice
¾ teaspoon salt
1 teaspoon paprika
1 teaspoon coriander seed, crushed
1 teaspoon cardamom seed, crushed (discard shells)
Parsley sprigs

1. Place salmon and shrimp in a shallow glass dish. Mix remaining ingredients except parsley and pour over fish. Refrigerate covered 30 minutes; stir twice.
2. Transfer fish and marinade to a large skillet. Simmer covered 4 minutes; stir and simmer uncovered 2 minutes. Add shrimp to skillet; simmer covered just until shrimp are done (about 3 minutes). Arrange fish and shrimp on a serving platter. Spoon pan juices over. Garnish with parsley.

*6 to 8 servings*

## Sole with Shrimp Pâté in Champagne

*Fillets are rolled with asparagus and a filling of shrimp, creamy cheese, and anchovy. Poached in champagne and served with our version of hollandaise sauce, this entrée is just right for special occasions.*

*1 pound fresh asparagus, spears only (2-inch pieces)
Fish Stock (page 26)
8 sole fillets (about 3 pounds)
2 cups cooked, shelled shrimp
2 ounces Neufchatel cheese
2 teaspoons anchovy paste
1 cup champagne or Fish Stock
1 cup Mock Hollandaise Sauce (page 22)
Lemon wedges

1. Simmer asparagus spears in 1 inch of stock 4 minutes; drain. Set aside.
2. Lay fillets on a flat surface. Purée shrimp with cheese and anchovy paste in a food processor or blender. Spoon shrimp mixture in center of fillets.
3. Arrange asparagus on shrimp mixture in center of fillets so spears are visible on sides; roll fillets and place seam side down in a large skillet. Pour champagne into skillet; simmer covered until fish is tender and flakes with a fork (about 5 minutes). Remove fish carefully with a slotted spoon to serving platter. Spoon hollandaise sauce over fillets; garnish with lemon wedges.

*8 servings*

*Frozen asparagus spears can be substituted for the fresh. Thaw and drain; do not cook.

# Steamed Red Snapper Oriental

*Soy sauce and sesame oil lend a distinctive Oriental flavor to this lively dish.*

3 red snapper (about 1½ pounds each), drawn and scaled
5 garlic cloves, finely sliced
   Fish Stock (page 26)
1 cup light soy sauce
½ cup dry white wine
3 tablespoons peanut or vegetable oil
1 tablespoon sesame oil
1 bunch green onions, tops only, cut in 2-inch matchstick-size pieces
*½ teaspoon freshly ground Szechuan or black pepper
3 zucchini slices
3 thin carrot slices
3 cloves
   Lemon or lime slices
   Watercress

1. Place fish on a piece of cheesecloth which is 18 inches longer than the fish. Using cheesecloth, lower fish onto rack in a fish steamer or large, deep roasting pan with 1½ inches of stock in bottom. Arrange garlic slices on fish. Simmer covered until fish is tender and flakes with a fork (about 40 minutes).
2. Using cheesecloth, lift fish from steamer to a heated platter. Remove cheesecloth from fish, carefully lifting fish with spatula and cutting cheesecloth with scissors if necessary.
3. Mix soy sauce, wine, and peanut and sesame oils in a small saucepan; heat to boiling. Drizzle 3 tablespoons soy mixture over fish; arrange green onion tops decoratively on fish. Sprinkle ground pepper over fish. Place zucchini and carrot slices over eyes of fish and secure with cloves. Arrange lemon slices and watercress around fish. Pass remaining soy mixture to spoon over individual servings.
4. If desired, let fish stand 45 minutes after poaching, then refrigerate until chilled (about 4 hours). Spoon hot soy mixture over fish and garnish as directed. Pass remaining soy mixture.

*8 to 10 servings*

*Note:* Whole white fish, lake trout, or other lean fish can be substituted for the red snapper.

*Lightly roast Szechuan pepper over medium heat in skillet before grinding.

# Baked Fish with Red Sauce

*The sauce, made with puréed red peppers, is piquant and distinctive.*

*2 pounds haddock fillets, cut in serving-size pieces
1 teaspoon salt
¼ teaspoon freshly ground white pepper
1 lemon, thinly sliced
1 medium red onion, sliced
4 large sweet red peppers, cut in quarters
¼ cup dry vermouth
½ teaspoon salt
   Dry vermouth
   Watercress

1. Sprinkle haddock with 1 teaspoon salt and the pepper; place in a lightly oiled baking pan. Arrange lemon, onion, and peppers over fish. Pour ¼ cup vermouth over top.
2. Bake at 350°F about 20 minutes, or until fish is tender and flakes with a fork.
3. Place peppers and onion slices in a food processor or blender container; discard lemon. Arrange fish on serving platter; keep warm.
4. Purée peppers, onion, and salt, adding additional vermouth, if needed, to make a thick sauce. Heat mixture thoroughly; spoon over fish. Garnish with watercress.

*6 servings*

*Flounder, halibut, or whitefish fillets, or poultry can be used in this recipe.

# Chilled Decorated Whitefish

1 whole whitefish (about 5 pounds), dressed
Fish Stock (page 26)
2 cups minced celery
2 cups minced carrot
2 hard-cooked eggs, minced
¾ teaspoon salt
⅛ teaspoon freshly ground white pepper
1⅓ cups Mock Mayonnaise (page 22)
1 cup sliced carrot
1 cup ¼- to ⅛-inch strips red or green pepper
1 green olive slice
2 lemons, thinly sliced
Selection of sauces: Light Green Sauce, Seasoned Dark Green Sauce, Citrus Mayonnaise, Mock Hollandaise Sauce (pages 21, 20, 23, 22)

1. Place fish on a piece of cheesecloth which is 18 inches longer than the fish. Using cheesecloth, lower fish onto rack in a fish steamer or a large, deep roasting pan with 1½ inches stock in bottom. Simmer covered until fish is tender and flakes with a fork (about 40 minutes). Using cheesecloth, lift fish from steamer. Let cool to room temperature. Carefully remove skin and transfer fish to a serving platter.

2. Stir celery, minced carrot, eggs, salt, and pepper into mayonnaise. Form the head and tail and fins of the fish, using the vegetable-mayonnaise mixture. Decorate the head and fins with the carrot slices. Decorate the tail and gills with strips of pepper. Place an olive slice in position for the eye. Garnish fish with lemon slices. Refrigerate until chilled (about 2 hours). Serve with 2 or 3 of the sauces.

*8 to 10 servings*

# Crab-Stuffed Trout with Tarragon

*The flavor of onions, mushrooms, crab meat, and tarragon permeates the trout while baking. Use fresh tarragon if it is available.*

2 large onions, finely chopped
¼ cup dry white wine
1 cup sliced fresh mushrooms
8 ounces fresh or 1 can (7¾ ounces) chunk crab meat, drained and flaked
1 tablespoon snipped fresh or 1½ teaspoons dried tarragon leaves
¼ cup snipped parsley
½ teaspoon salt
¼ teaspoon freshly ground white pepper
6 dressed trout (1 to 1½ pounds each)
1 tablespoon snipped fresh or 1½ teaspoons dried tarragon leaves
Lemon twists

1. Simmer onion in wine until tender (about 5 minutes). Mix 1½ cups cooked onion with the mushrooms, crab meat, 1 tablespoon tarragon, the parsley, salt, and pepper. Stuff trout with onion mixture.

2. Spread remaining onion in a shallow baking pan; arrange trout over onion.

3. Bake at 400°F about 20 minutes, or until fish is tender and flakes with a fork. Remove fish to serving platter. Sprinkle with 1 tablespoon tarragon and garnish with lemon twists.

*6 servings*

## Sole Véronique in Parchment

*Baked in parchment paper, the fish retains its natural moisture and flavor.*

2 pounds sole fillets
¾ teaspoon salt
3 tablespoons snipped parsley
2 teaspoons minced lemon peel
1½ cups seedless white grapes
⅔ cup dry white wine
   Lemon wedges

1. Lay each fillet on a piece of parchment paper or aluminum foil, 12x12 inches. Sprinkle fillets with salt, parsley, and lemon peel. Divide grapes over fish; sprinkle with wine. Bring edges of parchment up, crimp edges and seal; place on a jelly-roll pan.
2. Bake at 350°F 20 minutes.
3. Place parchment packets on individual plates; let each person open packet. Serve with lemon wedges.

*4 servings*

## Fish Stew

*French fish stew (bouillabaisse) is traditionally made with a selection of fresh shellfish. Our version uses fish which is more available and less expensive. Add shellfish if you like.*

*3 pounds fish fillets, skinned
5 medium tomatoes, peeled and chopped
3 carrots, chopped
1 large onion, thinly sliced
2 teaspoons salt
¼ teaspoon freshly ground pepper
2 garlic cloves, minced
1 teaspoon fennel seed, crushed
1 tablespoon minced orange peel
1 cup dry white wine
1 quart Fish Stock (page 26)

1. Cut fish into 1½-inch pieces. Set aside.
2. Simmer tomatoes, carrots, onion, salt, pepper, garlic, fennel, and orange peel in a mixture of wine and stock 15 minutes. Add fish to stock mixture; simmer covered until fish is tender and flakes with a fork (about 20 minutes).
3. Serve immediately in large shallow soup bowls.

*8 servings (2 cups each)*

*Flounder, haddock, cod, whitefish, halibut, bass, or other fish can be used in this recipe. For maximum flavor and variety, select at least 3 kinds of fish.

## Crab Meat Soup with Sherry

1 cup 1-inch celery pieces
1⅓ cups Fish Stock (page 26)
2 cans (7¾ ounces each) crab meat, drained (reserve 1 cup flaked crab meat)
½ cup instant nonfat dry-milk solids
½ cup water
½ cup whole milk
¼ teaspoon salt
⅛ teaspoon ground mace
4 teaspoons arrowroot
   Cold water
2 tablespoons dry sherry
3 tablespoons finely sliced celery for garnish

1. Simmer celery in stock in a covered saucepan 15 minutes. Place celery and stock in a food processor or blender; add 1 cup of flaked crab meat, the milk solids, water, milk, salt, and mace. Purée mixture; pour back into saucepan.
2. Heat crab mixture to simmering. Mix arrowroot with a little cold water; stir into crab mixture. Simmer, stirring constantly, until mixture has thickened. Stir in sherry and remaining crab meat. Heat thoroughly. Garnish with celery slices. Serve immediately.

*4 servings (1½ cups each)*

# Oysters Rockefeller

*No cream, eggs, or bread crumbs in this version of a popular classic.*

- **1 pint oysters**
- ***2 pounds fresh spinach, washed and stems removed**
- **1 cup instant nonfat dry-milk solids**
- **2 tablespoons chopped onion**
- **2 garlic cloves, minced**
- **1 teaspoon salt**
- **¼ teaspoon freshly ground pepper**
- **⅛ teaspoon freshly ground nutmeg**
- **2 egg whites**
- **⅓ cup grated Jarlsberg or Parmesan cheese**

1. Drain oysters; reserve liquor. Cook spinach in a covered saucepan with water clinging to leaves until tender (about 7 minutes); drain. Purée spinach with reserved liquor, the milk solids, onion, garlic, salt, pepper, nutmeg, and egg whites in a food processor or blender. Pour mixture into a saucepan; heat thoroughly.

2. Layer half the spinach mixture into large shell dishes or ramekins. Top with oysters; spoon remaining spinach mixture over oysters. Sprinkle with cheese. Set on a cookie sheet.

3. Bake at 400°F about 10 minutes, or until bubbly. Broil 1 to 2 minutes to brown tops. Serve immediately.

*4 servings*

*Note:* This recipe will make 8 first-course servings. Prepare recipe as directed; serve in shell-shaped ramekins or custard cups.

*If desired, substitute 2 packages (10 ounces each) frozen chopped spinach for fresh; cook following package directions.

# Bay Scallops with Cucumber Rings

*Serve this entrée in a clear bowl so that the layering is visible.*

- **2 pounds bay scallops or sea scallops, cut in thirds**
- **1 tablespoon minced onion**
- **½ cup minced celery**
- **1 cup minced carrot**
- **1½ cups Chicken Stock (page 25)**
- **½ teaspoon salt**
- **2 large cucumbers, pared, sliced lengthwise, seeded, and cut in 1-inch slices**
- **¼ cup dry white wine**
- **1 tablespoon arrowroot**
  **Cold water**
  **Salt**

1. Simmer scallops, onion, celery, and carrot in the stock until scallops are tender (about 4 minutes). Strain stock into a medium saucepan. Sprinkle ½ teaspoon salt over scallop mixture; keep warm.

2. Simmer cucumbers in stock until just tender (about 4 minutes). Remove cucumbers with slotted spoon; keep warm.

3. Heat remaining stock and wine to boiling. Mix arrowroot with a little cold water; stir into stock. Simmer, stirring constantly, until thickened (about 3 minutes). Season to taste with salt. Spoon half the cucumbers into a clear glass serving bowl. Arrange scallops on top. Spoon remaining cucumbers over scallops; pour sauce over. Serve immediately.

*6 servings*

# Gingered Scallops

3 cups Fish Stock (page 26)
1 tablespoon minced fresh ginger root
2 tablespoons dry sherry
½ teaspoon ground ginger
1½ pounds bay scallops or sea scallops, cut in ½-inch pieces
¾ cup chopped celery
2 teaspoons arrowroot
Cold water
Salt
Snipped parsley

1. Combine stock and ginger root in a medium skillet. Simmer until stock is reduced to 1 cup (about 15 minutes). Strain stock and discard ginger root. Return stock to skillet; stir in sherry and ground ginger.
2. Simmer scallops and celery in stock until tender (about 4 minutes). Remove scallops with a slotted spoon to small shell dishes. Mix arrowroot with a little cold water; stir into stock. Simmer, stirring constantly, until sauce is thickened (about 2 minutes). Taste and season with salt. Spoon sauce over scallops; sprinkle with parsley.

*4 servings*

*Note:* This recipe will make 6 first-course servings.

# Herbed Shrimp in Beer

*Simmer the shrimp in the marinade instead of broiling them, if you desire. Also excellent served as an appetizer with Mock Hollandaise Sauce (page 22) or Cucumber Sauce (page 21) for dipping.*

2 pounds peeled raw shrimp
1½ cups beer
2 teaspoons lemon juice
2 garlic cloves, minced
2 tablespoons snipped chives
2 tablespoons snipped parsley
1½ teaspoons salt
½ teaspoon freshly ground pepper
Shredded lettuce
2 green onions, finely chopped

1. Combine all ingredients except lettuce and green onions in a bowl. Refrigerate covered 8 hours or overnight; stir occasionally. Drain; reserve marinade.
2. Broil shrimp 4 inches from heat until cooked and tender (about 2 minutes on each side; less time for small shrimp). Do not overcook or shrimp will become tough. Brush occasionally with marinade. Marinade can be heated and served for dipping, if desired.
3. Serve shrimp on shredded lettuce; sprinkle with chopped green onion.

*6 servings*

# Citrus Seafood Salad

*Seafood and citrus flavors team for a refreshing salad entrée.*

3 cups shredded iceberg lettuce
½ cup Citrus Mayonnaise (page 23)
1 teaspoon celery seed
1½ pounds cooked crab meat, lobster, flounder, or whitefish, cut in ½-inch pieces
Salt
Freshly ground white pepper
1 navel orange, sliced

Arrange lettuce on a serving platter or individual plates. Mix Citrus Mayonnaise and celery seed; gently fold fish into mixture. Mound fish mixture on lettuce; sprinkle very lightly with salt and pepper. Arrange orange slices around fish mixture.

*4 servings*

# Mock Crab Meat Salad

*You will hardly be able to tell that the crab meat is mock, but use fresh fish and cook it carefully.*

1¾ pounds halibut steaks
1 cup Fish Stock (page 26)
½ cup dry white wine
1 teaspoon salt
¼ teaspoon freshly ground
   white pepper
2 tablespoons snipped fresh or 2
   teaspoons dried dill weed
¾ cup Mock Mayonnaise (page
   22)
   Lettuce leaves
4 rings cut from honeydew or
   cantaloupe
½ pound white grapes
1 lime, cut in 4 wedges

1. Simmer halibut in stock and wine in a large skillet until fish is tender and flakes with a fork (about 10 minutes). Remove fish from skillet; let cool to room temperature. Discard skin and bones.

2. Flake two thirds of the fish; cut remaining fish into ½-inch pieces. Stir salt, pepper, and dill into mayonnaise. Mix flaked fish into ½ cup of the mayonnaise; mix fish pieces into remaining mayonnaise.

3. Arrange lettuce leaves on 4 individual salad plates; place melon rings on lettuce. Mound flaked fish mixture inside melon rings; top with mixture of fish pieces. Garnish salads with clusters of grapes and lime wedges.

*4 servings*

*Note:* This recipe makes 8 first-course servings. Prepare recipe as directed except substitute melon pieces for the melon rings, increase grapes to ¾ pound, and use 2 limes for wedges.

# POULTRY

Poultry is important in both new and old French cooking, perhaps because it is plentiful in France and because its flavor weds so nicely with a whole gamut of sauces.

Chicken, Cornish hens, turkey, capon, and chicken livers are used in a variety of delectable ways in this chapter. In keeping with the new principles, sauces are very flavorful, but not rich in fat. Vegetable purée provides the thickening, sometimes arrowroot or cornstarch is used, and other times just the pan juices are spooned over poultry.

The stuffings that are used are not heavy with bread. Instead, vegetables become the primary ingredients.

Duck is a fatty bird, but the recipes here tell you how to get rid of the fat. In one recipe, the skin and fat are removed from the uncooked duck; then the surface is covered with grape leaves during roasting. At the end, bread crumbs are spread on the surface and the duck is placed under the broiler to brown. In another recipe, the cooked duck is served cold after removing skin and fat.

# Cornish Hens Normandy

*These tempting hens are roasted on a bed of onions and apples with a sprinkling of cinnamon.*

4 Cornish hens (1 to 1¼ pounds each), cut in halves
Chicken Stock (page 25)
1 large yellow onion, chopped
¼ cup Madeira wine or Chicken Stock
1 cinnamon stick, broken in half
4 tart cooking apples, cut in ½-inch slices
Watercress

1. Rinse hens; pat dry. Place hens skin side up on a broiler pan. Broil 4 inches from heat 15 minutes, basting with stock several times.
2. Simmer onion in wine with cinnamon stick 5 minutes. Arrange onion in bottom of a shallow baking pan; discard cinnamon stick. Arrange apple slices over onions; place hens on apples.
3. Roast in a 350°F oven about 45 minutes, or until hens are tender. Arrange hens and apple mixture on a platter; garnish with watercress.

*4 servings*

# Cornish Hens with Raisin Stuffing

*Plumped raisins and rice are the base of the stuffing. Grapevine leaves cover the breasts of the Cornish hens to retain moistness.*

4 Cornish hens (1 to 1½ pounds each)
Salt
*16 grapevine leaves preserved in brine
⅔ cup dark raisins
⅓ cup brandy
¾ cup cooked long-grain rice
1¼ cups finely chopped carrot
1¼ cups finely chopped celery
½ teaspoon cinnamon
1 tablespoon clarified butter
¼ teaspoon salt
⅛ teaspoon pepper
½ cup brandy

1. Rinse hens and pat dry; sprinkle lightly with salt.
2. Soak grapevine leaves in cold water 20 minutes. Pat dry. Set aside.
3. Simmer raisins in brandy 15 minutes; remove from heat and let stand 15 minutes. Stir in rice, carrot, celery, cinnamon, clarified butter, ¼ teaspoon salt, and the pepper. Spoon stuffing lightly into cavities of hens. Place hens on rack in a roasting pan. Cover breasts with grapevine leaves.
4. Roast in a 325°F oven 1¼ to 1½ hours, or until hens are tender. Baste with brandy during last ½ hour of roasting. Let hens stand 15 minutes before serving. Remove grapevine leaves.

*4 servings*

*Grapevine leaves can be purchased in a gourmet shop or in the specialty department of a supermarket.

# Roast Chicken Tarragon

*Based on the classic French recipe, the sauce is made without whipping cream, flour, and eggs. It is delicately flavored with tarragon and spooned over roasted chicken.*

1 **broiler-fryer chicken (2½ to 3 pounds)**
2 **teaspoons clarified butter**
2 **teaspoons snipped fresh or 1 teaspoon dried tarragon leaves**
  **Salt**
2 **carrots, cut in 1-inch pieces**
1 **small onion, cut in quarters**
1 **stalk celery, cut in 1-inch pieces**
2 **sprigs parsley**
1¼ **cups Chicken Stock (page 25)**
1 **tablespoon arrowroot**
  **Cold water**
½ **teaspoon salt**
¼ **teaspoon freshly ground white pepper**
2 **teaspoons snipped fresh or 1 teaspoon dried tarragon leaves**
2 **tablespoons dry sherry**

1. Rinse chicken; pat dry. Place in a roasting pan. Brush chicken with clarified butter, sprinkle with 2 teaspoons tarragon. Sprinkle cavity with salt; fill cavity with carrot, onion, celery, and parsley.
2. Roast in a 325°F oven about 2½ hours, or until chicken is done; meat on drumstick will be very tender. Remove chicken to a platter. Remove vegetables; reserve. Cover loosely with aluminum foil and let stand 20 minutes before carving.
3. Spoon fat from roasting pan. Heat stock to simmering in roasting pan, stirring to incorporate particles from pan. Mix arrowroot with a little cold water; stir into stock with salt, pepper, 2 teaspoons tarragon, and the sherry. Simmer, stirring constantly, until stock is thickened (about 5 minutes).
4. Slice chicken and arrange on platter. Garnish with reserved vegetables. Serve with sauce.

*4 servings*

# Chicken with Poached Garlic

*The garlic, poached without peeling, imparts a delicate flavor to the chicken.*

1 **broiler-fryer chicken (2½ to 3 pounds)**
1 **garlic clove, peeled and cut in half**
  **Juice of 1 lime**
  **Salt**
  **Freshly ground white pepper**
16 **garlic cloves (unpeeled)**
½ **cup Chicken Stock (page 25)**
¼ **cup dry vermouth**
  **Chicken Stock**
2 **teaspoons arrowroot**
  **Cold water**
¼ **cup Mock Crème Fraîche (page 18)**
1 **tablespoon snipped parsley**
  **Salt**
  **Freshly ground white pepper**

1. Rinse chicken; pat dry. Place in a roasting pan. Rub entire surface of chicken with cut garlic clove. Squeeze lime juice over chicken. Sprinkle cavity and outside of chicken lightly with salt and pepper. Place remaining garlic cloves around chicken; pour in ½ cup stock and ¼ cup dry vermouth.
2. Roast in a 325°F oven about 2½ hours, or until done; meat on drumstick will be very tender. Add stock if necessary to keep garlic covered. Remove chicken to platter. Cover loosely with aluminum foil. Let stand 20 minutes before carving.
3. Spoon fat from roasting pan. Add enough stock to pan to make 1 cup of liquid. Mix arrowroot with a little cold water; stir into stock. Simmer, stirring constantly, until thickened (about 3 minutes). Stir in Mock Crème Fraîche and parsley. Season to taste with salt and pepper. Pass sauce with chicken.

*4 servings*

*Note:* To eat garlic cloves, gently press with fingers; the soft cooked interior will slip out. The flavor of the poached garlic is very delicate.

# Chicken en Cocotte

1½ cups sliced leeks, white part
    only
1 medium zucchini, cut in
    ¼-inch slices
2 large sweet red or green
    peppers, cut in ¼-inch strips
1 large green pepper, cut in
    ¼-inch strips
2 teaspoons snipped fresh or 1
    teaspoon finely crushed dried
    rosemary leaves
2 teaspoons snipped fresh or 1
    teaspoon finely crushed dried
    thyme leaves
1½ teaspoons salt
⅓ cup dry sauterne or other
    white wine
1 roasting chicken (about 3
    pounds)
1 teaspoon clarified butter
    Salt
1 small bunch parsley
1 cup 3-inch pieces leek, green
    part only
1 tablespoon dry sauterne or
    other white wine

1. Arrange 1½ cups leeks, the zucchini, and peppers in bottom of a Dutch oven. Mix rosemary, thyme, and 1½ teaspoons salt; sprinkle one third of herb mixture over vegetables. Pour ⅓ cup sauterne over vegetables.
2. Rinse chicken and pat dry. Rub chicken with butter and sprinkle with remaining herb mixture. Lightly salt cavity of chicken. Stuff cavity with parsley and green part of leeks; sprinkle with 1 tablespoon sauterne. Place chicken in Dutch oven; cover with lid.
3. Bake at 325°F 2 hours, or until tender. Remove chicken to platter; discard parsley and leek from cavity. Surround chicken with vegetables.

*4 servings*

# Roast Turkey with Pineapple-Stuffed Breast

*A stuffing of pineapple, cooked poultry, and curry is carefully spread beneath the skin of the turkey breast so that the flavors are absorbed while roasting.*

1 turkey (10 to 12 pounds)
1½ tablespoons curry powder
2 teaspoons salt
⅓ cup minced onion
4 garlic cloves, minced
1 teaspoon minced ginger root
2 tablespoons vegetable oil
⅔ cup unsweetened pineapple
    juice
1 can (20 ounces) unsweetened
    crushed pineapple, drained
1½ cups minced cooked turkey or
    chicken
    Unsweetened pineapple juice

1. Rinse turkey; pat dry. Carefully loosen skin over turkey breast by running fingers under the skin.
2. Mix curry powder, salt, onion, garlic, ginger root, vegetable oil, and ⅔ cup pineapple juice. Mix one quarter of the spice mixture with the drained pineapple and minced turkey. Spread pineapple mixture gently and evenly under skin of turkey breast with fingers. Place turkey in a roasting pan. Insert meat thermometer in thickest part of thigh. Brush remaining spice mixture over turkey breast.
3. Roast in a 325°F oven until thermometer registers 175°F (3½ to 4 hours); baste occasionally with pineapple juice. Remove turkey to serving platter; cover loosely with aluminum foil. Let stand 20 minutes before carving.

*About 16 servings*

*Note:* This recipe can be used for a roasting chicken of about 5 pounds. Use half the spice and pineapple mixtures; proceed as directed. Roast at 325°F about 2½ hours, or until chicken is tender; drumstick meat will feel very soft.

# Capon with Vegetable Dressing

*The intriguing combination of vegetables gives the impression of an old-time stuffing.*

1 capon (about 5 pounds)
½ can (10½-ounce size) condensed onion soup
1 medium eggplant, pared and cut in ½-inch cubes
1 cup chopped onion
1 cup chopped celery
1 cup chopped carrot
1½ to 2 teaspoons salt
¼ teaspoon freshly ground pepper
2 teaspoons poultry seasoning
¼ cup snipped parsley
2 eggs, beaten

1. Rinse capon; pat dry with paper toweling. Place capon on rack in a roasting pan. Pour onion soup over.
2. Roast in a 325°F oven about 2½ hours, or until capon is done; meat on drumstick will be very tender.
3. Remove capon to a serving platter; let stand 15 minutes before carving.
4. While capon is roasting, simmer eggplant in 1 inch of **salted water** until tender (about 10 minutes); drain.
5. Process onion, celery, and carrot in a food processor or blender until finely ground; transfer mixture to a mixing bowl. Mix in eggplant and remaining ingredients. Spoon vegetable mixture into a lightly oiled 2-quart casserole; do not cover.
6. Bake at 325°F 45 minutes. Remove to serving bowl.

*4 servings*

*Note:* Do not bake vegetable dressing in cavity of capon because the correct texture will not be obtained.

This dressing is excellent served with pork.

# Capon Roasted in Salt

*The salt casing leaves the chicken lean, moist, and tender with just a tinge of salt flavor.*

1 capon (about 5 pounds)
Salt
1 carrot, cut in 1-inch pieces
1 medium onion, cut in quarters
2 sprigs parsley
6 to 7 pounds coarse kosher salt
Watercress

1. Rinse capon; pat dry. Salt inside of cavity lightly; fill cavity with vegetables.
2. Line a deep Dutch oven (that will fit size of capon, allowing 1½ to 2 inches space on bottom, sides, and top) with heavy-duty aluminum foil, allowing 2 inches of foil to fold down over top edge of pan. Fill bottom of Dutch oven with a 1½-inch layer of salt. Place capon in Dutch oven. Carefully fill Dutch oven with salt, being careful not to get salt inside cavity of capon. Layer salt over top of capon.
3. Roast uncovered in a 400°F oven 2 hours. Remove from oven. Let stand 15 minutes.
4. Lay Dutch oven on its side. Using foil lining, gently pull salt-encased capon from Dutch oven. Break salt from capon, using an ice pick or screwdriver and hammer. Place capon on serving platter; remove vegetables from cavity. Garnish with watercress. Serve immediately.

*4 servings*

# Chicken Meringue

*Meringue replaces the need for a pastry crust in this colorful chicken pot pie.*

10 tiny boiling onions
2 stalks celery, cut in 1-inch pieces
1 large sweet red pepper, cut in ½-inch pieces
2 carrots, cut in ½-inch slices
2 cups Chicken Stock (page 25)
4 cups cubed cooked chicken
½ pound medium mushrooms, cut in half
½ pound fresh pea pods, or 1 package (10 ounces) frozen pea pods, thawed
2 tablespoons cornstarch
Cold water
Salt
Freshly ground pepper
4 egg whites
½ teaspoon salt
¼ teaspoon cream of tartar
1 tablespoon snipped fresh or 1½ teaspoons dried chervil leaves
2 tablespoons instant nonfat dry-milk solids

1. Simmer onions, celery, red pepper, and carrot in stock until just tender (about 8 minutes). Remove vegetables with slotted spoon and mix with chicken, mushrooms, and pea pods in a 2-quart casserole.
2. Mix cornstarch with a little cold water. Stir into stock: simmer, stirring constantly, until mixture thickens (about 4 minutes). Season to taste with salt and pepper. Pour over chicken in casserole.
3. Bake covered at 350°F 15 minutes.
4. Beat egg whites and ½ teaspoon salt until foamy. Add cream of tartar and chervil; continue beating, adding dry-milk solids gradually, until egg whites form stiff but not dry peaks. Spread meringue over casserole mixture, sealing to edges of casserole.
5. Bake at 350°F 12 to 14 minutes, or until meringue is lightly browned. Serve immediately.

*4 to 6 servings*

# Chicken Livers Marsala

*Green pepper, onion, and water chestnuts provide crisp contrast to the smooth texture of the chicken livers.*

1 cup diced green pepper
½ cup finely chopped onion
⅔ cup water chestnuts, sliced in half
1½ cups Chicken Stock (page 25)
¼ cup Marsala wine
1½ pounds chicken livers, cut in half (discard membrane)
2 teaspoons arrowroot
Cold water
½ teaspoon bottled brown bouquet sauce
Salt
Freshly ground pepper
Parsley sprigs

1. Simmer green pepper, onion, and water chestnuts in stock and wine until tender (about 5 minutes). Remove from stock with slotted spoon; keep warm. Add chicken livers to stock; simmer until livers are tender (about 8 minutes). Remove livers from stock with slotted spoon; add to vegetables and keep warm.
2. Mix arrowroot with a little cold water. Stir into stock. Simmer, stirring constantly, until it thickens (about 3 minutes). Stir brown bouquet sauce, vegetables. and livers into sauce. Season with salt and pepper to taste. Heat until hot. Spoon into ramekins. Garnish with parsley. Serve at once.

*4 servings*

# Vegetable-Stuffed Chicken Breasts

*Chicken breasts are rolled around a flavorful vegetable mixture and baked with creamy Cauliflower Sauce and Swiss cheese—elegant for entertaining.*

3 whole large chicken breasts (about 3 pounds), boned, halved, and skinned
¾ pound cauliflower
¼ pound broccoli
Chicken Stock (page 25)
½ cup finely chopped celery
2 shallots, minced
½ teaspoon salt
Cauliflower Sauce (page 19; do not add cheese or parsley)
3 ounces Swiss cheese, shredded
Snipped parsley

1. Rinse chicken breasts; pat dry. Pound with mallet until even in thickness; set aside.
2. Remove leaves and tough stalks from cauliflower and broccoli; separate into flowerets. Simmer covered in 1 inch of stock until tender (about 8 minutes). Coarsely chop the cauliflower and broccoli; mix with the celery, shallots, and salt.
3. Spoon mixture onto chicken breasts; roll up carefully and place seam side down in a lightly oiled shallow baking pan. Spoon Cauliflower Sauce over breasts.
4. Bake covered at 350°F 40 minutes. Uncover and bake 15 minutes. Sprinkle cheese over breasts; bake until cheese is melted (about 5 minutes). Arrange chicken on platter; sprinkle with parsley.

*6 servings*

# Curried Breast of Chicken Salad

6 cups bite-size pieces cooked chicken
1½ cups sliced celery
1 can (8½ ounces) water chestnuts, drained and cut in thirds
½ teaspoon salt
¼ teaspoon finely ground pepper
1 cup Mock Mayonnaise (page 22)
1 teaspoon curry powder
2 tablespoons dry sherry
Lettuce leaves
Orange slices

1. Combine chicken, celery, water chestnuts, salt, and pepper.
2. Mix Mock Mayonnaise, curry, and sherry; stir gently into chicken mixture. Serve on lettuce-lined plates; garnish with orange slices.

*6 servings*

# Ducklings with Green Peppercorn Sauce

2 ducklings (about 4½ pounds each)
1½ teaspoons salt
¼ teaspoon freshly ground pepper
1 teaspoon snipped fresh or ½ teaspoon dried crumbled rosemary leaves
Chicken Stock (page 25)
Green Peppercorn Sauce (page 20)

1. Rinse ducklings; pat dry. Place ducklings breast side up on rack in a roasting pan. Sprinkle with salt, pepper, and rosemary. Pierce breasts of ducklings with a fork several times.
2. Roast in a 350°F oven about 2½ hours, or until ducklings are done; drumstick meat will feel very tender. Baste ducklings occasionally with stock. Remove ducklings to a serving platter; let stand 15 minutes before carving.
3. Serve with the sauce.

*6 to 8 servings*

# Duckling with Fruit Salad

2 ducklings (about 4½ pounds each)
2 teaspoons salt
½ teaspoon freshly ground pepper
¾ teaspoon allspice
½ cup fruit juice
6 slices fresh or canned pineapple
6 preserved kumquats, thinly sliced
3 oranges, peeled and segments removed
2 apples, sliced
2 papayas, peeled and sliced, if desired
2 bananas, sliced
1 pound white grapes
1 lime, cut in 6 wedges
1 lemon, cut in 6 wedges
1½ cups Low-Fat Yogurt (page 19)
2 tablespoons snipped mint
Mint sprigs

1. Rinse ducklings; pat dry. Place ducklings breast side up on rack in a roasting pan. Sprinkle with salt, pepper, and allspice. Pierce breasts of ducklings with a fork several times.
2. Roast in a 350°F oven about 2½ hours, or until ducklings are done; drumstick meat will feel very soft. Baste ducklings occasionally with fruit juice. Remove ducklings to platter; let cool.
3. While ducklings are roasting, prepare fruits; refrigerate. Mix yogurt and snipped mint; refrigerate.
4. Carefully cut skin and fat from ducklings. Remove meat from carcass carefully, keeping meat in as large pieces as possible. Arrange duckling meat and fruits attractively on individual plates. Garnish with mint. Pass chilled yogurt sauce.

*6 servings*

# Crumb-Crusted Duckling Halves

*The ducklings are covered with grapevine leaves to insure moistness. A delicious crumb coating adds crispness. Serve with a variety of sauces.*

*16 grapevine leaves preserved in brine
2 ducklings (about 4½ pounds each), cut in half
2 teaspoons salt
½ cup Chicken Stock (page 25)
Juice of 1 lemon
Clarified butter
⅓ cup seasoned stuffing crumbs, slightly crushed
Cumberland Sauce (page 22) or Madeira Sauce (page 23)

1. Soak grapevine leaves in cold water 20 minutes. Pat dry. Set aside.
2. Using fingers and a sharp knife, remove skin and excess fat from ducklings (do not skin wings). Place ducklings breast side up on rack in a roasting pan; sprinkle with salt. Cover surface of ducks with grapevine leaves.
3. Roast in a 325°F oven about 2½ hours, or until ducklings are done; drumstick meat will feel soft. Baste ducklings every half hour with a mixture of stock and lemon juice.
4. Remove grapevine leaves. Brush ducklings very lightly with butter and sprinkle with crumbs. Broil 4 inches from heat until crumbs are browned (about 5 minutes). Remove ducklings to platter; let stand 10 minutes before serving. Serve with desired sauce.

*4 servings*

*Grapevine leaves can be purchased in a gourmet shop or in the specialty section of a supermarket.

# VEGETABLES

Vegetables often take a prominent position in the New French cuisine. A wide range of vegetables is used, and they are prepared in many innovative ways. The emphasis is on naturalness and achieving the maximum in flavor. Vegetables are always cooked from the fresh state; thus knowing what is in season is important. It is better to substitute a different vegetable in the recipe than to resort to using a canned or frozen version.

When you shop for vegetables, choose a market that you know specializes in offering vegetables at their peak of freshness. They should be young, tender, and sweet—not old, blemished, or held at warm temperatures. The cooler the vegetable stays during transport, the fresher and sweeter it will taste. After you buy vegetables, hurry them home to the vegetable bin of your refrigerator and use them promptly.

Go easy on the cooking of the vegetables. The idea is to cook them until they are just crisp-tender and not a moment more. At this point they are at the peak of flavor and color. Additional cooking or holding in a covered pot hastens flavor loss, off colors, and mushy texture.

If your main dish is elaborate and features an important sauce, you probably should keep the accompanying vegetables plain or just lightly adorned. But even if they are plain, arrange them in an artistic manner on a platter or as an eye-catching garnish for the meat. French chefs always take great pride in their creative vegetable displays.

With main dishes that are not sauced or have just a light glaze, a sauced vegetable dish is appropriate. But remember to keep it light and low in fat. A number of attractive sauced vegetable dishes appear in this chapter. Also see pages 18–26.

## Asparagus Extraordinaire

1½ pounds fresh asparagus
 1 medium sweet red pepper, cut
    in ¼-inch strips
   Chicken Stock (page 25)
   Salt
   Freshly ground pepper
 ¼ pound prosciutto or boiled
    ham, cut in 1x⅛-inch strips
 ½ cup Mock Hollandaise Sauce
    (page 22)

1. Break off and discard tough parts of asparagus stalks. Pare stalks. Simmer asparagus and pepper strips in 1 inch of stock in a covered skillet until tender (about 7 minutes); drain.
2. Arrange asparagus spears on a serving platter; arrange pepper strips over center of asparagus. Sprinkle lightly with salt and pepper. Arrange ham along sides of asparagus. Spoon hollandaise over all.

*4 servings*

*Note:* For a special luncheon entrée, increase amount of asparagus to 2 pounds and the ham to ½ pound. Arrange on individual plates; top each with a **poached egg**.

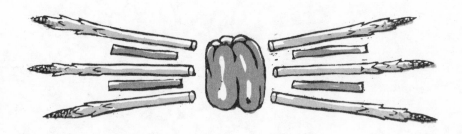

# Herbed Cabbage

3 cups shredded cabbage
1 large onion, sliced
½ teaspoon snipped fresh or ¼ teaspoon dried tarragon leaves
½ teaspoon snipped fresh or ¼ teaspoon dried basil leaves
2 teaspoons snipped fresh or 1 teaspoon dried marjoram leaves
¼ teaspoon freshly ground pepper
Chicken Stock (page 25)
2 teaspoons clarified butter
½ pound mushrooms, sliced
1 teaspoon salt
Snipped parsley

1. Place cabbage and onion in a medium saucepan: sprinkle with tarragon, basil, marjoram, and pepper. Pour in 1 inch of stock; simmer covered until cabbage is tender (about 10 minutes). Drain.
2. Heat butter in a medium skillet until bubbly; add mushrooms and cook 4 minutes, stirring occasionally. Stir mushrooms and salt into cabbage mixture. Sprinkle with snipped parsley. Serve with Mock Crème Fraîche (page 18) or yogurt, if desired.

*4 to 6 servings*

# Herbed Stuffed Mushrooms

*¾ pound mushrooms, chopped
¼ teaspoon salt
⅛ teaspoon freshly ground pepper
1½ teaspoons snipped fresh or ½ teaspoon dried basil leaves
1 tablespoon snipped parsley
½ cup chopped onion
8 large mushrooms, stems removed and sliced into rounds; reserve caps
2 tablespoons brandy
1 tablespoon clarified butter
Parsley for garnish (optional)

1. Process ¾ pound mushrooms, the salt, pepper, basil, parsley, and onion in a food processor or blender until thick and smooth. Layer ½ cup of the mushroom mixture in bottom of a baking dish.
2. Mix sliced mushroom stems, brandy, and butter. Fill reserved mushroom caps with mixture; place filled caps in baking dish. Spoon remaining mushroom mixture around mushrooms.
3. Bake at 400°F 20 minutes. Garnish with parsley.

*4 servings*

*Note:* This recipe is also excellent for a first course.

*If desired, chop mushrooms in food processor or blender, following manufacturer's directions.

# French-Style Peas

2 cups shelled peas (see Note)
8 small boiling onions, cut in half
1 cup shredded lettuce
1 teaspoon sugar
2 teaspoons snipped parsley
2 teaspoons clarified butter
½ teaspoon salt
¼ teaspoon freshly ground pepper
¾ cup water

Combine all ingredients except water; let stand 1 hour, stirring occasionally. Transfer mixture to a saucepan; add water. Simmer covered until peas and onions are tender (about 15 minutes). Serve hot.

*4 servings*

*Note:* Two packages (10 ounces each) frozen peas can be substituted in this recipe; do not mix with other ingredients. Add to saucepan during last 5 minutes of cooking.

# Whipped Carrots with Dill

1 pound carrots, sliced
Chicken Stock (page 25)
½ cup Mock Crème Fraîche (page 18)
2 tablespoons snipped fresh or 1 tablespoon dried dill weed
1 teaspoon salt

1. Simmer carrots in 1 inch of stock in a covered saucepan until tender (about 15 minutes); drain.
2. Purée in a food processor or blender with remaining ingredients. Return to saucepan; heat thoroughly.

*4 servings*

# Whipped Carrots and Pears

*Vegetables no longer need to be dull or monotonous; this unexpected combination proves how exciting they can be.*

1 pound carrots, sliced
Chicken Stock (page 25)
2 medium pears, pared, cored, and chopped
½ cup Citrus Mayonnaise (page 23)
¼ teaspoon salt
1 teaspoon toasted sesame seed

1. Simmer carrots in 1 inch of stock in a covered saucepan until tender (about 10 minutes); drain.
2. Purée in a food processor or blender with pears, mayonnaise, and salt. Return to saucepan; heat thoroughly. Sprinkle with sesame seed.

*6 servings*

# Stewed Okra and Tomatoes

1 pound okra, cut in 1-inch pieces
4 medium onions, chopped
4 large tomatoes, cored and chopped (see Note)
½ cup Beef Stock (page 25)
2 tablespoons fresh lemon juice
½ teaspoon coriander seed, crushed
1 teaspoon salt
¼ teaspoon freshly ground pepper
Lemon wedges

Combine all ingredients except lemon wedges in a medium saucepan. Simmer covered over low heat 45 minutes. Serve hot, or refrigerate and serve cold. Accompany with lemon wedges.

*6 to 8 servings*

*Note:* If fully ripe fresh tomatoes are not available, use drained tomatoes from a 29-ounce can.

# Squash and Tomatoes Parmesan

2 large yellow squash, pared and
    cut in thirds lengthwise
    Chicken Stock (page 25)
¾ teaspoon salt
¼ teaspoon freshly ground
    pepper
1½ teaspoons snipped fresh or ¾
    teaspoon dried basil leaves
1½ teaspoons snipped fresh or ¾
    teaspoon dried oregano
    leaves
¼ teaspoon garlic powder
3 medium tomatoes, cut in thin
    slices
3 tablespoons freshly grated
    Parmesan cheese

1. Simmer squash in a large covered skillet in 1 inch stock until tender (about 8 minutes).
2. Remove squash to broiler pan. Sprinkle with half the salt, pepper, basil, oregano, and garlic. Top squash with tomato slices; sprinkle with remaining spices and cheese.
3. Broil 3 inches from heat until cheese browns (3 to 5 minutes).

*6 servings*

# Broiled Tomatoes with Piquant Sauce

*Serve this versatile recipe as a first course, too.*

6 medium tomatoes, cut in half
    Salt
    Freshly ground pepper
1 hard-cooked egg, minced
1 egg, slightly beaten
1 tablespoon wine vinegar
1 tablespoon Worcestershire
    sauce
1 teaspoon curry powder
½ teaspoon sugar
½ teaspoon dry mustard
3 tablespoons low-fat ricotta
    cheese
½ teaspoon salt
¼ cup water

1. Arrange tomatoes cut side up on a broiler pan. Season with salt and pepper. Broil 5 inches from heat 8 minutes.
2. Mix remaining ingredients except water in top of a double boiler. Cook and stir over simmering water 2 minutes; add ¼ cup water. Stir until sauce has thickened (about 3 minutes). Spoon sauce over tomatoes.

*6 servings*

*Note:* The sauce in this recipe can be served over any cooked vegetables. It is also delicious over steaks or roast beef.

# Cauliflower with Seasoned Dark Green Sauce

1 medium head cauliflower
    Chicken Stock (page 25)
    Juice of ½ lemon
    Fresh spinach leaves
1 cup Seasoned Dark Green
    Sauce (page 20)

1. Remove leaves and tough parts of stalks from cauliflower. Place whole cauliflower in a deep saucepan. Pour in 2 inches of stock and the lemon juice. Simmer covered until cauliflower is tender (20 to 25 minutes). Drain and remove cauliflower to a platter.
2. Arrange spinach leaves on platter. Pour sauce over cauliflower. Cut into wedges to serve.

*6 servings*

# Brussels Sprouts and Grapes

1½ pounds fresh Brussels sprouts,
    cut in half
1½ cups beer
  2 teaspoons clarified butter
  ¼ teaspoon salt
  ⅛ teaspoon freshly ground white
    pepper
  1 cup seedless white grapes
    Snipped parsley

1. Simmer Brussels sprouts in beer in covered saucepan until tender (about 8 minutes); drain.
2. Drizzle butter over sprouts; sprinkle with salt and pepper. Add grapes; heat thoroughly. Sprinkle with parsley.

*4 to 6 servings*

# Green Onions with Mock Hollandaise

  4 bunches green onions, cleaned
    and trimmed
1¼ cups Chicken Stock (page 25)
    Salt
  ⅔ cup Mock Hollandaise Sauce
    (page 22)
  ¼ teaspoon freshly grated nutmeg
    Orange wedges

1. Arrange green onions in a large skillet; pour stock over. Simmer until onions are tender (about 10 minutes). Drain; arrange onions on a platter; sprinkle lightly with salt.
2. Blend hollandaise and nutmeg. Serve over onions. Garnish platter with orange wedges.

*4 to 6 servings*

# Baked Cheddar Onions

  6 medium onions
  3 cups chopped carrots
1½ cups (6 ounces) shredded
    Cheddar cheese
  1 teaspoon thyme
  ½ teaspoon salt
    Chicken Stock (page 25)

1. Cut a thin slice off both ends of each onion; peel. Carefully scoop out inside of onions with a sharp knife or melon-baller, leaving a shell 2 or 3 rings thick. Chop onion centers; mix with carrots, cheese, thyme, and salt. Fill onions with mixture; place in a shallow baking pan. Pour ½ inch stock around onions.
2. Bake at 400°F 1 to 1¼ hours, or until onions are tender.

*6 servings*

*Note:* This recipe is also excellent served as a first course.

# Zucchini Squares

*Mint and zucchini are an interesting and refreshing combination. Cut into smaller squares, the mixture can be served as a first course.*

1 pound zucchini, shredded
2 teaspoons salt
4 ounces feta cheese, crumbled
2 eggs, beaten
2 teaspoons flour
2 teaspoons snipped fresh or 1
  teaspoon crumbled dried
  mint leaves
¼ cup finely chopped green onion
  tops
¼ teaspoon freshly ground
  pepper
1 cup Low-Fat Yogurt (page 19)
1 teaspoon snipped fresh or ½
  teaspoon crumbled dried
  mint leaves

1. Mix zucchini with 2 teaspoons salt. Let stand 10 minutes; rinse and drain well between paper toweling. Mix zucchini with remaining ingredients except yogurt and 1 teaspoon mint. Beat mixture well with a fork. Pour mixture into a lightly oiled 8-inch square baking pan.
2. Bake at 375°F 45 minutes. If further browning is desired, place under broiler 1 minute. Cut into squares to serve.
3. Mix yogurt and 1 teaspoon snipped mint. Serve over zucchini squares.

*6 to 8 servings*

*Note:* **Dill weed** can be substituted for the mint in this recipe, using the same amounts.

# Gingered Turnips

*Oriental seasonings give this often neglected vegetable new flavor appeal.*

2 pounds yellow turnips, pared
  and cubed
1 tablespoon minced onion
1¼ cups Beef Stock (page 25)
½ teaspoon ground ginger
½ teaspoon sugar
2 teaspoons soy sauce

Combine all ingredients in a saucepan; simmer covered until turnips are tender (about 15 minutes). Drain; mash turnips with potato masher or electric mixer until fluffy, adding cooking liquid as needed for desired consistency.

*6 servings*

# Composed Vegetable Platter

*Eye appeal promotes appetite appeal—add other fresh vegetables if desired.*

1 large sweet red pepper, cut in
  1-inch pieces
3 large green peppers, sliced
3 medium kohlrabi, pared, cut in
  half lengthwise, and sliced
6 carrots, sliced
  Chicken Stock (page 25)
  Herbed Mock Mayonnaise
  (page 22)

1. Simmer vegetables in a covered saucepan in 1 inch of stock just until tender (about 10 minutes). Drain.
2. Arrange red pepper pieces in center of a large round platter. Arrange remaining vegetables in circles around the red pepper. Pass the mayonnaise or spoon over vegetables.
3. The vegetable platter can be refrigerated and served cold as a salad.

*8 servings*

*Note:* You may desire to serve 2 or 3 sauces with the vegetable platter; Cucumber Sauce, Seasoned Dark Green Sauce, and Green Onion Sauce (pages 21, 20, 23) would be excellent.

# Vegetable-Stuffed Grapevine Leaves

*For a Greek accent, serve this tasty vegetable combination with a lamb entrée.*

1 small eggplant, pared and cut in ¼-inch cubes
Water
⅔ cup chopped onion
⅔ cup chopped celery
⅔ cup chopped carrot
1¼ teaspoons salt
¼ teaspoon freshly ground pepper
½ teaspoon poultry seasoning
½ teaspoon cinnamon
2 tablespoons snipped parsley
2 teaspoons snipped fresh or 1 teaspoon dried mint leaves
*1 jar (8 ounces) grapevine leaves preserved in brine
Cold water
1 cup water
2 tablespoons fresh lemon juice
¾ cup Mock Hollandaise Sauce (page 22)

1. Simmer eggplant in 1 inch of salted water in a covered saucepan until tender (about 10 minutes); drain.
2. Process onion, celery, and carrot in a food processor or blender until finely ground; transfer mixture to mixing bowl. Mix in eggplant, salt, pepper, poultry seasoning, cinnamon, parsley, and mint. Spoon vegetable mixture into a 1-quart casserole.
3. Bake at 325°F 40 minutes; cool slightly.
4. Soak grapevine leaves in cold water 20 minutes; pat dry. Cover bottom of large skillet with four leaves. Place a rounded tablespoon of vegetable mixture on stem end of each leaf; roll up leaf, tucking in sides. Place filled leaf seam side down in skillet. Repeat with remaining leaves and vegetable mixture.
5. Pour 1 cup water and the lemon juice over rolls. Simmer covered 30 to 35 minutes. Serve hot, or refrigerate and serve cold. Pass hollandaise. This recipe can also be served as a first course.

*8 servings (4 rolls each)*

Note: **Low-Fat Yogurt** (page 19) can be used in place of the Mock Hollandaise Sauce.

*Grapevine leaves can be purchased in a gourmet shop or in the specialty department of a supermarket.

# Soy Pilaf with Fresh Vegetables

*A Middle Eastern influence is found in the ingredients of this unusual recipe.*

1½ cups chopped onion
½ cup soy grits or granules (see Note)
1 small eggplant, pared and cut in ½-inch cubes
1½ cups Chicken Stock (page 25)
½ teaspoon curry powder
¼ teaspoon salt
½ teaspoon paprika
½ teaspoon cumin
¼ teaspoon chili powder
⅛ teaspoon garlic powder
¼ teaspoon salt
2 medium tomatoes, chopped
1 green onion, chopped
1½ tablespoons lemon juice
¼ teaspoon salt
⅛ teaspoon freshly ground pepper
1 tablespoon snipped parsley

1. Spread onion in a 9x5x2-inch baking dish; sprinkle with soy. Layer eggplant over top. Mix stock with curry, salt, paprika, cumin, chili powder, and garlic; pour over eggplant.
2. Bake covered at 350°F 1 hour. Mound mixture on a serving platter; sprinkle with ¼ teaspoon salt.
3. While eggplant mixture is baking, mix tomatoes and remaining ingredients in a small bowl. Refrigerate covered. Spoon around pilaf on platter.

*4 to 6 servings*

Note: Soy grits can be purchased in specialty or health food stores. They have a flavor similar to cracked wheat.

Cracked wheat can be used in this recipe. You will need **2 cups cooked cracked wheat;** cook according to package directions.

# Vegetable Mélange

*In our version of scalloped tomatoes, eggplant replaces the bread cubes.*

1 medium eggplant, pared and
    cut in ¾-inch pieces
1 can (16 ounces) tomatoes, cut
    in thirds; use juice
4 stalks celery, cut in ¾-inch
    pieces
½ cup snipped parsley
½ cup dry vermouth
1½ teaspoons salt
¼ teaspoon freshly ground
    pepper
2 tablespoons snipped fresh or
    1½ teaspoons dried fennel
    leaves
1 cup coarsely chopped onion
1½ cups coarsely chopped green
    pepper

Combine all ingredients except onion and green pepper in a Dutch oven; simmer covered 30 minutes. Add onion and green pepper; simmer uncovered 20 minutes, stirring occasionally. Serve in small bowls.

*6 to 8 servings*

*Note:* Try different herb combinations in place of the fennel: **2 teaspoons snipped fresh basil** and **1 teaspoon snipped fresh oregano,** or **2 teaspoons curry powder** and **1 teaspoon cumin.**

# Vegetable Casserole Niçoise

½ head iceberg lettuce, cut in
    2-inch pieces
3 tomatoes, cut in quarters
4 heads Belgian endive, cut in
    ½-inch slices
½ cup ripe olives, sliced
4 slices prosciutto or 2 slices
    boiled ham, cut in 2x⅛x⅛-inch
    strips
4 anchovies, minced
½ teaspoon salt
¼ teaspoon freshly ground
    pepper
¾ cup Beef Stock (page 25)
¼ cup dry white wine or Beef
    Stock
¼ cup grated Gruyère cheese

1. Arrange lettuce, tomatoes, and endive in a 9x5x2-inch casserole. Sprinkle with olives, prosciutto, anchovies, salt, and pepper. Pour stock and wine over all.
2. Bake at 350°F 25 minutes. Sprinkle with cheese and bake until cheese is melted (about 5 minutes).

*6 to 8 servings*

# Vegetable Kabobs

*Colorful vegetables, threaded on a skewer and covered with Cauliflower Sauce, make an elegant presentation.*

24 Brussels sprouts
 2 small zucchini, each cut in 6
    pieces
   Chicken Stock (page 25)
12 cherry tomatoes
12 mushrooms
   Salt
1⅓ cups Cauliflower Sauce (page
    19)

1. Simmer Brussels sprouts and zucchini in 1 inch of stock in a covered saucepan 5 minutes. Drain vegetables; cool.
2. Thread vegetables alternately on skewers. Sprinkle lightly with salt. Arrange kabobs in a shallow baking dish.
3. Bake at 400°F about 10 to 15 minutes, or until vegetables are tender; baste occasionally with stock. Serve hot sauce over kabobs.

*6 servings*

# SALADS
## AND DRESSINGS

While not prominent in French cuisine, salads are at least important enough to be served as a separate course in both the old and new styles of cooking. Special care is always taken to create an attractive plate to set before guests.

A French salad is not just a bowl of iceberg lettuce tossed with dressing. It is a pleasing array of well-chilled ingredients, usually featuring several crisp greens plus contrasting vegetable ingredients.

For a classic French meal, the salad is served as a palate refresher following the main course. For a New French dinner, you can vary this rigid rule and serve the salad before the main course, after it, or even as the first course. But do serve it separately.

Classic salads never contain fruits and they would *never* be a sweet molded gelatin concoction—the kind so popular on American buffet tables. (The French do serve gelatins, but they are likely to be pretty, nonsweet aspics served as appetizers. Gelatin also goes into the various mousses and Bavarian crèmes.)

A New French salad would still not be a sweet gelatin dish, but you will find a few with fruits. There is much more room for experimentation, and you will even find influences from the Orient, Greece, Italy, Germany, America, the Middle East, and French country cooking.

This chapter offers a cornucopia of ideas for you. Some of the salad recipes here have their own dressings. Others refer you to dressings and Mock Crème Fraîche (page 18).

Salads made of greens and vegetables are quite low in calories; it is the salad dressings that make the calorie count climb. The basic French dressing is two thirds oil and one third vinegar. Mayonnaise-type dressings are even richer. In this book the dressings have been lightened by replacing some of the oil with other liquids. Ingredients such as fresh basil, mint, caraway seed, onion, soy sauce, and lemon contribute flavor appeal. Mock Crème Fraîche and low-fat yogurt are used to shed many calories from creamy dressings.

# Green Bean and Onion Salad

1 pound small boiling onions
1½ pounds fresh green beans
Chicken Stock (page 25)
½ cup Mock Crème Fraîche (page 18)
¼ cup low-fat cottage cheese
2 tablespoons snipped fresh chives
1 teaspoon snipped fresh or ½ teaspoon dried thyme leaves
1 teaspoon snipped fresh or ½ teaspoon dried marjoram leaves
Salt
Freshly ground pepper
Juice of ½ lemon

1. Simmer onions and beans in 1 inch of stock in a covered saucepan until tender (15 to 18 minutes). Drain; refrigerate covered until chilled (about 2 hours).
2. Mix remaining ingredients except salt, pepper, and lemon juice; refrigerate covered until chilled.
3. Arrange vegetables on a platter; sprinkle lightly with salt and pepper. Squeeze lemon juice over. Spoon sauce over or pass sauce separately.

*6 servings*

# Fresh Bean Sprout Salad

*A crisp, colorful, light salad.*

1 pound fresh bean sprouts, rinsed (see Note)
2 medium carrots, shredded
1 tablespoon toasted sesame seed
2 teaspoons vegetable oil
⅓ cup distilled white vinegar
2 teaspoons sugar

1. Mix bean sprouts and carrots in a shallow glass dish.
2. Shake remaining ingredients in a covered jar; pour over vegetables.
3. Refrigerate covered 1½ hours; stir occasionally. Serve in shallow bowls.

*4 to 6 servings*

*Note:* If fresh bean sprouts are not available, you can substitute 1 large pared, seeded, shredded cucumber.

# Beet Mousse

*Both elegant and unusual, this salad is worth the effort to make. Try as a first course, too.*

8 medium beets
1 tablespoon vinegar
1½ teaspoons unflavored gelatin
¼ cup orange juice
½ cup instant nonfat dry-milk
   solids
2 to 3 ice cubes
1½ teaspoons prepared horseradish
   Salad greens

1. Cut greens from beets; discard. Simmer beets in 2 inches water and vinegar until tender (about 30 minutes). Slip off skins. Cut thin slice from bottoms of beets; hollow out centers with melon-baller, leaving ½-inch shells; reserve centers. Refrigerate beets until chilled.
2. Sprinkle gelatin over orange juice in a small saucepan; let stand 5 minutes. Set over low heat, stirring occasionally, until gelatin is dissolved (about 3 minutes). Pour gelatin mixture into a food processor or blender; add beet centers and dry-milk solids. Process, adding ice cubes one at a time, until mixture is the consistency of thick whipped cream. Stir in horseradish. Fill beets with mixture; refrigerate until serving time. Serve on salad greens.

*4 servings*

# Red Cabbage-Apple Salad

*In this cross between coleslaw and Waldorf salad, you will enjoy crisp textures and tart flavors.*

3 cups shredded red cabbage
1 red apple, cut in 1½x¼-inch
   strips
1 sweet red pepper, cut in
   1½x¼-inch strips
2 tablespoons cider vinegar
¼ cup apple juice
¼ teaspoon caraway seed
⅛ teaspoon salt
⅛ teaspoon freshly ground
   pepper
   Salad greens

Mix all ingredients except salad greens in a medium bowl. Refrigerate covered 2 hours. Serve on salad greens on individual plates.

*4 servings*

# Raw Broccoli Salad

*If you have never eaten broccoli raw, you have a treat in store.*

3 cups raw bite-size pieces
   broccoli spears
½ cup Low-Fat Yogurt (page 19)
½ teaspoon salt
¼ teaspoon freshly ground
   pepper
2 ounces Cheddar cheese,
   shredded
1 large carrot, cut in thin slices

Mix broccoli with yogurt, salt, and pepper. Spoon mixture on 4 salad plates. Sprinkle tops of salads with cheese; arrange carrot slices around salads.

*4 servings*

*Note:* See recipe for Garden Vegetables in Sweet Seasoned Vinegar (page 79) to use broccoli stalks.

## Fresh Spinach Salad

*This is an example of a composed salad, where ingredients have been carefully arranged for eye and appetite appeal.*

**4 cups bite-size pieces spinach**
**1 cup ½-inch pieces yellow
     squash**
**1 can (7¾ ounces) water
     chestnuts, drained and sliced**
**2 hard-cooked eggs, chopped**
**½ cup sliced green onions
     Salt
     Freshly ground pepper**
**½ cup Mustard Sauce (page 32)**
**½ cup Low-Fat Yogurt (page 19)**

Arrange spinach, squash, water chestnuts, eggs, and onion attractively in rows on a medium platter; sprinkle lightly with salt and pepper. Mix Mustard Sauce and yogurt; drizzle over salad.

*6 servings*

*Note:* This recipe will make 4 luncheon servings with the addition of **2 cups flaked tuna.**

## Greek Salad in Peppers

*The natural juice from the tomato and the lemon juice are the "salad dressing" for this salad. Add a dollop of yogurt, if desired.*

**1 large tomato, chopped**
**1 green onion, sliced**
**⅛ teaspoon salt**
**1 teaspoon snipped fresh or ½
     teaspoon dried basil leaves**
**1 tablespoon fresh lemon juice**
**4 small green peppers, cored**
**½ cup crumbled feta cheese**
**8 anchovies, drained and rinsed**
**8 lemon wedges**

1. Mix tomato, onion, salt, basil, and lemon juice; refrigerate covered 1 hour.
2. Spoon half the tomato mixture into green peppers; layer cheese over tomatoes. Spoon remaining tomato mixture over cheese. Arrange 2 anchovies over top of each pepper. Serve with lemon wedges.

*4 servings*

## Cucumbers with Buttermilk Dressing

**1 medium cucumber, pared,
     seeded, and finely chopped**
**1 teaspoon salt**
**1 tablespoon fresh lemon juice**
**1 tablespoon Mock Crème
     Fraîche (page 18)**
**¾ cup buttermilk**
**1 tablespoon snipped fresh or 1
     teaspoon dried dill weed**
**½ teaspoon salt**
**⅛ teaspoon freshly ground
     pepper**
**1 cucumber, sliced**
**2 large tomatoes, sliced**

1. Sprinkle chopped cucumber with 1 teaspoon salt; let stand 10 minutes. Rinse cucumber; pat dry and place in a mixing bowl. Mix lemon juice, crème fraîche, buttermilk, dill, ½ teaspoon salt, and the pepper; pour over cucumber and refrigerate covered 1 hour.
2. Arrange sliced cucumber and tomatoes on individual plates; spoon buttermilk mixture over.

*4 servings*

*Note:* This recipe can be increased and served as a first-course soup; stir in skim milk if thinner consistency is desired.

# Fruited Carrot Salad

*Tart apple pieces would be an interesting addition to this salad.*

4 carrots
1 cup unsweetened pineapple juice
2½ cups orange juice
Lettuce cups
Snipped mint

1. Pare carrots into strips with a vegetable peeler. Place in a shallow glass dish; pour fruit juices over. Refrigerate covered 6 hours or overnight, stirring occasionally.
2. Drain carrots, spoon into lettuce cups, and garnish with mint.

*4 servings*

# Oriental Cucumber Salad

10 baby cucumbers (about 3 inches long), sliced in very thin rounds
1 bunch green onions, tops only, finely chopped
2 teaspoons honey or sugar
2 teaspoons toasted sesame seed
½ cup distilled white vinegar
½ teaspoon sesame oil
5 tablespoons light soy sauce
Salad greens

1. Arrange cucumber and onion in a shallow glass dish. Shake remaining ingredients except salad greens in a covered jar; pour over the vegetables. Refrigerate for 2 hours, stirring occasionally.
2. Drain cucumber and onion; marinade can be strained and refrigerated for use again. Serve salad on lettuce or other salad greens.

*4 servings*

# Garden Vegetables in Sweet Seasoned Vinegar

1½ cups very thinly sliced baby cucumbers
2 cups very thinly sliced broccoli stalks
½ cup cider vinegar
½ teaspoon salt
¼ teaspoon freshly ground pepper
1½ teaspoons sugar
Salad greens

1. Arrange vegetable slices in a shallow glass dish. Shake remaining ingredients except salad greens in a covered jar; pour over vegetables. Refrigerate covered 30 minutes; stir occasionally. Drain; marinade can be strained and refrigerated for use again.
2. Serve vegetables on salad greens.

*4 servings*

# Vegetable Salad with Yogurt Dressing

*Vivid colors dominate this unusual salad combination.*

¾ cup Low-Fat Yogurt (page 19)
2 tablespoons snipped parsley
½ cup finely chopped dill pickle
½ cup chopped tomato
1 teaspoon salt
1 cup sliced radishes
1 medium zucchini, shredded
2 medium carrots, shredded
1 large beet, shredded

1. Mix yogurt, parsley, pickle, chopped tomato, and salt; refrigerate covered 1 hour.
2. Arrange radish slices around edge of a serving plate. Arrange zucchini, carrots, and beet decoratively in center of plate. Serve yogurt mixture with salad.

*4 servings*

# Vegetable Platter Vinaigrette

*Use any fresh vegetables that you want in this recipe—let your imagination be your guide.*

1 pound fresh green beans
1 small head cauliflower
  Chicken Stock (page 25)
1 cup Vinaigrette Dressing (page 24)
1 pint cherry tomatoes, halved
  Salt
  Freshly ground pepper
1 medium red onion, thinly sliced

1. Steam green beans and whole cauliflower in separate covered saucepans in 1 inch of stock until tender (about 15 minutes). Drain. Mix beans with ½ cup dressing and refrigerate covered 3 hours, stirring occasionally. Refrigerate cauliflower. Mix cherry tomatoes with ½ cup dressing; refrigerate covered 3 hours, stirring occasionally.
2. Drain beans and tomatoes; reserve dressing. Place cauliflower in center of a platter; arrange beans and tomatoes around cauliflower. Sprinkle vegetables lightly with salt and pepper. Arrange onion slices over beans and tomatoes. Cut cauliflower into wedges to serve. Pass reserved dressing.

*8 to 10 servings*

# Red Vegetable Salad

1 pint cherry tomatoes, stems removed, cut in half
20 radishes, sliced
1 small red onion, sliced
3 tablespoons wine vinegar
2 teaspoons salad oil
1 teaspoon salt
2 teaspoons snipped fresh mint
⅛ teaspoon freshly ground white pepper
  Lettuce leaves

1. Combine all ingredients except lettuce leaves in a medium bowl; refrigerate covered 2 hours, stirring occasionally.
2. Serve vegetables on lettuce.

*4 to 6 servings*

# Pineapple-Mint Salad

1 can (20 ounces) unsweetened pineapple chunks, drained
2 cups low-fat cottage cheese
½ bunch mint, snipped
  Bibb lettuce
1 cup sliced celery
  Mint sprigs
8 orange slices

1. Dice 1 cup of the pineapple; mix with cottage cheese and snipped mint.
2. Arrange lettuce leaves on a platter or individual plates; mound pineapple mixture on lettuce. Arrange remaining pineapple and the celery around mounds of pineapple mixture. Garnish with mint sprigs and orange slices.

*4 to 6 servings*

# California Fruit Plate

*Fresh fruits are a must for this recipe. If figs and raspberries are not available, substitute other ingredients such as strawberries and melon.*

2 cups low-fat cottage cheese
8 fresh figs, cut in quarters
2 cups fresh raspberries
2 tablespoons honey
4 lemon wedges

Place ½ cup cottage cheese on each of 4 salad plates. Surround cottage cheese with 8 quarters of fig; sprinkle raspberries over figs. Drizzle honey over fruit and cottage cheese. Squeeze lemon over all.

*4 servings*

Molded Cheese Dessert, 83; Fresh Fruit with Brandy Cream, 84; Pineapple-Berry Dessert, 84

# DESSERTS

Desserts do not have to leave you feeling guilty after you have eaten them, nor must you groan as you push yourself away from the table. You also don't have to be a martyr while telling everyone, "But I never eat desserts!"

It is possible for desserts to be delicious, nutritious, refreshing, and moderately low in calories as well as fun to eat. It's all a part of the pleasures you can gain from eating the New French way.

You can start by ignoring many of the classic creations that are elaborate, showy, and full of butter, sugar, and heavy cream. They are time-consuming to make, and most people aren't hungry enough to eat them after a complete dinner. Rich cakes, pies, tarts, Bavarian crèmes, ice cream, and gooey syrups should go by the wayside.

Meals end so nicely with just a sampling of homemade fruit sherbet, a low-fat mousse, baked fruit in wine, a tart made without pastry, or fresh fruit topped with Mock Crème Fraîche. Recipes for these light and tantalizing desserts appear in this chapter, along with others equally pleasing.

## Dessert Puff with Fruit

*A fancy "show-off" dessert to impress family and friends.*

- 4 eggs, slightly beaten
- ¾ cup skim milk
- ¾ cup flour
- 2 teaspoons sugar
- ¼ teaspoon salt
- 2 teaspoons clarified butter
- 4 cups assorted sliced fruits
- 1 cup Low-Fat Yogurt (page 19)
  Freshly ground nutmeg

1. Combine eggs, milk, flour, sugar, and salt; beat with a fork until blended but still slightly lumpy. Heat butter in a 10-inch skillet until bubbly and sides of skillet are hot; pour batter into skillet.
2. Bake at 425°F 20 minutes. Turn oven control to 350°F; bake until golden (10 to 15 minutes). (Do not open oven door during baking. Sides of puff will rise very high; the center will rise only slightly.) Remove from oven and cut into 8 wedges; place on individual plates.
3. Spoon ½ cup fresh fruit on each wedge. Dollop fruit with yogurt; sprinkle with nutmeg. Serve immediately.

*8 servings*

## Squash and Apple Confection

*Apple and squash slices form a decorative pattern in this molded dessert. Try it also as a meat accompaniment.*

- 3 large Golden Delicious apples
- 1 cup prune juice
- 1 cup water
- ¾ teaspoon ground ginger
- 3 eggs, beaten
- 1½ pounds acorn squash or pumpkin, pared and sliced
  Chicken Stock (page 25)
- 3 tablespoons currants or dark raisins
- 1¼ cups Custard Sauce (page 25)

1. Cut each apple into 12 slices; layer slices in a medium skillet. Pour prune juice, water, and ginger over. Simmer covered 5 minutes. Drain, pouring liquid into a small mixing bowl. Stir eggs into liquid.
2. Cook squash in 1 inch of stock in a covered saucepan until tender (about 5 minutes); drain.
3. Alternate half the apple and squash slices in rows in bottom of a lightly oiled 9x5x3-inch loaf pan. Sprinkle with currants; layer remaining apple and squash slices on top. Pour egg mixture over top. Place pan in larger baking pan; fill with 1 inch boiling water.
4. Bake at 375°F about 45 minutes, or until set. Cool to room temperature. Refrigerate covered 2 hours. Run knife around edge of plate; unmold on a platter. Slice; serve sauce over slices.

*8 servings*

# Molded Cheese Dessert

*A not-too-sweet dessert with the unusual flavor of bay leaf.*

2 envelopes unflavored gelatin
1 cup cold water
1 cup double-strength coffee
1 pound pot cheese or low-fat
    cottage cheese
1 teaspoon vanilla extract
¼ cup sugar
2 bay leaves, broken in half
    Mint leaves or watercress

1. Sprinkle gelatin over cold water in a small skillet; let stand 5 minutes. Heat, stirring occasionally, over low heat until dissolved (about 3 minutes). Pour gelatin mixture into a food processor or blender; add remaining ingredients except bay leaves and mint. Purée mixture.
2. Spoon mixture into a 1-quart mold. Push bay leaf pieces into mixture. Refrigerate covered 4 to 6 hours; unmold. Garnish with mint.

*4 servings*

# Carrot-Apricot Tart

1 cup fresh or canned apricot
    halves, drained and cut into
    ¼-inch slices
1 pound baby carrots, cut in half
    lengthwise
½ teaspoon cinnamon
¾ cup carrot juice
2 eggs
½ cup instant nonfat dry-milk
    solids
¼ cup water
1 tablespoon brandy
¼ teaspoon nutmeg

1. Cover bottom of a 9-inch pie plate with apricots; arrange carrots in spoke design over apricots.
2. Mix remaining ingredients in a food processor or blender; pour over carrots.
3. Bake at 325°F about 45 minutes, or until set. Cool slightly. Cut into wedges to serve.

*6 servings*

# Cheese-Stuffed Strawberries

*A traditional French dessert, served in an elegant manner. If berries are small, slice them and serve the cheese mixture as a sauce.*

½ cup low-fat ricotta cheese
1 teaspoon grated lemon peel
1 teaspoon fresh lemon juice
1 teaspoon honey or sugar
48 large strawberries
    Mint sprigs (optional)

1. Mix cheese, lemon peel, lemon juice, and honey in a food processor or blender until fluffy; refrigerate until chilled (about 1 hour).
2. Gently scoop centers from strawberries with melon-baller or fruit knife. Fill with cheese mixture.
3. Arrange filled strawberries on small individual plates. Garnish with mint.

*4 servings*

# Pineapple-Berry Dessert

*Puréed strawberries are the sauce for this fruit dessert.*

1 large pineapple
½ cup light rum or orange juice
1 quart strawberries

1. Cut stem and end off pineapple; cut into quarters lengthwise. Remove core and pare; cut into ½-inch slices and place in a shallow glass dish. Pour rum over pineapple; refrigerate covered 4 hours, turning slices several times.
2. Arrange pineapple slices in overlapping pattern on a large platter.
3. Halve some of the strawberries and arrange on pineapple. Purée remaining strawberries in a food processor or blender and pour into a bowl. Serve with knife and fork.

# Fresh Fruit with Brandy Cream

½ cup Mock Crème Fraîche (page 18)
¼ cup low-fat ricotta cheese
2 teaspoons brandy or orange juice
¼ teaspoon ground ginger
2 teaspoons honey or sugar
3 cups assorted fresh fruit
2 teaspoons toasted sesame seed (optional)

1. Mix crème fraîche, ricotta, brandy, ginger, and honey in a food processor or blender until fluffy. Refrigerate until chilled (about 1 hour).
2. Arrange fruit on individual plates. Spoon sauce over; sprinkle with sesame seed.

*6 servings*

# Peaches and Cream

*Rice is the secret of this fanciful dessert served in pretty parfait glasses for an elegant effect.*

3 large ripe peaches, peeled
1½ teaspoons fresh lemon juice
½ cup long-grain rice
1 cup water
½ cup instant nonfat dry-milk solids
½ cup 2% milk
2 to 3 tablespoons honey or sugar
¼ teaspoon almond extract
Mint sprigs

1. Purée 2 of the peaches in a food processor or blender; stir in lemon juice. Coarsely chop remaining peach.
2. Cook rice according to package instructions. Purée rice with remaining ingredients except almond extract and mint in a food processor or blender. Simmer rice mixture in a saucepan over medium heat 8 minutes; stir constantly. Remove from heat; stir in almond extract.
3. Spoon rice mixture and peach purée alternately into stemmed parfait glasses. Top with chopped peaches. Garnish with mint. Serve warm, or refrigerate until chilled.

*6 servings*

*Note:* Substitute pears, strawberries, or other fresh fruit if peaches are not available.

# Baked Banana and Orange Compote

2 large navel oranges, peeled
½ teaspoon cinnamon
4 large bananas, peeled and cut
    in 1½-inch pieces
½ cup orange juice
    Cherries with stems

1. Cut oranges into ¼-inch slices; cut slices in half. Arrange orange slices in bottom of a shallow casserole; sprinkle with cinnamon.
2. Dip bananas in orange juice; arrange over oranges. Spoon remaining orange juice over fruit.
3. Bake at 400°F 15 minutes. Serve warm in compote dishes; garnish with cherries.

*6 servings*

*Note:* Serve with dollops of Mock Crème Fraîche (page 18), if desired.

# Baked Sherried Bananas

6 medium bananas, cut in half
    lengthwise and crosswise
    Pineapple juice
¼ cup sherry or pineapple juice
1 tablespoon honey
¼ teaspoon ground ginger
1 tablespoon toasted sesame seed

1. Dip bananas in pineapple juice; arrange in a shallow casserole. Spoon sherry and honey over bananas; sprinkle with ginger.
2. Bake at 400°F 15 minutes. Serve in shallow bowls; sprinkle with sesame seed.

*6 servings*

# Broiled Oranges

3 large navel oranges
3 tablespoons sweet vermouth
36 black cherries with stems

1. Cut oranges in half; cut around sections with fruit knife. Drizzle vermouth over oranges.
2. Broil 3 inches from heat until oranges are hot through (about 5 minutes).
3. Place one cherry in center of each orange half. Arrange remaining cherries around oranges on plates.

*6 servings*

# White Port Granite

*Serve this light, delicate dessert as a summer refresher.*

1 tray ice cubes (about 14)
¼ cup white port wine
    Juice of 1 lemon
1½ to 2 tablespoons sugar
    Lemon slices

1. Drop ice cubes, one at a time, into a food processor or blender, following manufacturer's directions. When ice is finely ground, add wine, lemon juice, and sugar. Process until ice is in small crystals.
2. Immediately spoon into stemmed glasses, garnish with lemon slices, and serve.

*4 servings (about ⅔ cup each)*

*Note:* This recipe is excellent served as a first course.

# Meringue Cakes with Fruit and Custard Sauce

4 egg whites (room temperature)
¼ teaspoon cream of tartar
¼ teaspoon salt
1½ tablespoons sugar
1½ tablespoons instant nonfat
    dry-milk solids
1 large pear, cut in ¼-inch cubes
¾ cup sliced strawberries
1 cup Custard Sauce (page 25)
6 strawberries

1. Beat egg whites until foamy. Add cream of tartar and salt; beat until stiff, but not dry, peaks are formed, adding sugar and dry-milk solids gradually.
2. Drop meringue by large rounded tablespoonfuls onto cookie sheet lined with brown paper.
3. Place in a 500°F oven; turn oven control to 300°F and bake 15 to 20 minutes, or until light brown. Remove from oven and let cool. Remove from cookie sheet.
4. Slice meringues crosswise in half. Stir pear cubes and sliced strawberries into sauce; spoon mixture into hollow bottom halves of meringues; place tops on meringues. Garnish with strawberries.

*6 servings (12 small meringues)*

# Sliced Poached Pears in Wine

½ cup Mock Crème Fraîche (page 18)
¾ cup puréed cherries
⅛ teaspoon ground cloves
4 large firm-ripe pears
3 cups water
2 tablespoons lemon juice
2 large sticks cinnamon, broken in 1-inch pieces
1½ cups white or pink Chablis wine
¼ teaspoon ground cloves

1. Mix crème fraîche, cherries, and ⅛ teaspoon ground cloves. Refrigerate covered 1 hour.
2. Cut pears in half lengthwise; remove cores. Cut halves carefully into thin slices, keeping halves together. Dip pear halves into a mixture of water and lemon juice; place halves close together in a medium saucepan. Tuck cinnamon sticks around pears; pour wine over. Sprinkle pears with ¼ teaspoon ground cloves.
3. Simmer covered until pears are just tender (12 to 15 minutes). Cool slightly. Arrange pears in shallow dishes, fanning slices out slightly. Serve warm, or refrigerate and serve cold. Pass crème fraîche or spoon over pears.

*8 servings*

*Note:* This recipe is also excellent served with Custard Sauce (page 25).

# Hot Apple-Raisin Compote

6 large apples, pared, cored, and cut in 1-inch pieces
½ cup golden raisins
1 stick cinnamon, broken in 3 pieces
⅔ cup water
1 tablespoon lemon juice
2 tablespoons bourbon
1 tablespoon chopped walnuts

1. Put apples, raisins, cinnamon stick, water, and lemon juice into a saucepan. Cook covered until apples are tender (about 10 minutes). Drain; discard cinnamon stick.
2. Add bourbon to saucepan; simmer until liquid is reduced by half. Purée 1 cup of the apples and raisins with liquid in a food processor or blender; pour mixture over remaining fruit and sprinkle with walnuts.

*8 servings*

# Basic Mousse with Variations

*Low in calories, yet superb in flavor, this adaptable recipe can be used to create your own variations.*

- 1 **envelope unflavored gelatin**
- ½ **cup cold water**
- 1 **cup instant nonfat dry-milk solids**
- ¼ **cup sugar or honey**
- 1 **teaspoon vanilla extract**
- 10 **to 12 ice cubes**
  **Mint sprigs or strawberries for garnish**

1. Sprinkle gelatin over cold water in a saucepan; let stand 5 minutes. Set over low heat, stirring constantly until gelatin is dissolved (about 3 minutes).
2. Pour gelatin mixture into a food processor or blender container; add remaining ingredients except ice cubes. Process 10 seconds. Add ice cubes one at a time until mixture has consistency of heavy whipped cream.
3. Pour mixture into a serving bowl or individual stemmed glasses. Refrigerate until set (about ½ hour). Garnish with mint or strawberries.

*6 servings*

*Note:* Mousse can be unmolded, if desired. Run knife around side of bowl; dip briefly in hot water. Invert on serving plate.

**Mocha Mousse:** Follow recipe for Basic Mousse, adding **1 tablespoon instant coffee crystals** and **¼ teaspoon ground cinnamon** to ingredients.

**Rum-Pineapple Mousse:** Follow recipe for Basic Mousse, adding **1 tablespoon dark rum** to ingredients. When mousse is almost consistency of heavy whipped cream, add **1 cup crushed pineapple.** Continue adding ice cubes until desired consistency is achieved.

**Ricotta Mousse:** Prepare half the Basic Mousse recipe. When desired consistency is reached, add **1 tablespoon apple concentrate, 1 cup low-fat ricotta cheese, and ¼ teaspoon cinnamon.** Turn food processor on and off 2 times so ingredients are just blended.

**Fruit Mousse:** Follow recipe for Basic Mousse, adding **1 cup sliced fruit or berries** to ingredients.

**Fruit Concentrate Mousse:** Follow recipe for Basic Mousse; omit sugar and add **3 tablespoons natural fruit concentrate** to ingredients. Garnish with slices of fresh fruit or **1 to 2 cups of prepared fruit.**

*Note:* Natural fruit concentrates can be purchased in specialty sections of the supermarket or in gourmet food shops. Many flavors, such as peach, apple, blackberry, and strawberry, are available.

# Banana-Sweet Potato Bake

1 cup mashed cooked sweet
    potato or squash
2 medium bananas
1 cup water
½ cup instant nonfat dry-milk
    solids
2 egg yolks
2 tablespoons honey or sugar
½ teaspoon ground ginger
2 tablespoons dark rum, if
    desired
4 egg whites
1 cup Custard Sauce (page 25)

1. Purée sweet potato, bananas, water, milk solids, egg yolks, honey, ginger, and rum in a food processor or blender. Pour into a mixing bowl.

2. Beat 4 egg whites until stiff but not dry peaks form. Fold into sweet potato mixture. Spoon into a lightly oiled 9x5x2-inch baking dish.

3. Bake at 325°F 45 minutes. Serve at room temperature, or refrigerate and serve cold. Cut into slices. Serve with Custard Sauce.

*6 servings*

# MENUS

# BRUNCH FOR GUESTS

*Champagne Punch*
*Pineapple-Berry Dessert (page 84)*
*Chicken Livers Marsala (page 62)*
*Puffy Omelet or Scrambled Eggs*
*Jellied Gazpacho (page 35)   Croissants*
*Coffee*

# ELEGANT LUNCHEONS

*Jellied Consommé (page 34)*
*Bay Scallops with Cucumber Rings (page 54)*
*Vegetable Platter Vinaigrette (page 80)*
*Moselle or Rhine Wine*
*Meringue Cakes with Fruit and Custard Sauce (page 86)*
———
*Pears with Roquefort (page 33)*
*Cold Roast Beef Vinaigrette (page 40)*
*Carrot Curls   Toast Fingers*
*Iced Tea*
*White Port Granite (page 85)*
———
*Spinach Soup with Onion Petals (page 35)*
*Curried Breast of Chicken Salad (page 63)*
*Oriental Cucumber Salad (page 79)*
*Vouvray Wine*
*Papaya-Mango Mousse (see Fruit Mousse, page 87)*
*or Pineapple-Berry Dessert (page 84)*
———
*Egg-Drop Soup (page 34)*
*Beef-on-Tomato Medallions (page 40)*
*Fresh Bean Sprout Salad (page 76)*
*Hot Tea*
*Rum-Pineapple Mousse (page 87)*
———
*Cold Artichoke Soup (see Artichoke Sauce, page 21)*
*Mock Crab Meat Salad (page 56)*
*Melba Rounds*
*Iced Tea*
*Molded Cheese Dessert (page 83)*

## FESTIVE OCCASION MEALS

*Jellied Consommé (page 34)*
*Oysters Rockefeller (page 54)*
*Light White Wine*
*Elegant Leg of Lamb (page 42)*
*Vegetable Kabobs (page 74; omit sauce)*
*Bordeaux Wine*
*Greens and Artichoke Heart Salad with Vinaigrette Dressing (page 24)*
*Papaya Mango Mousse (see Fruit Mousse, page 87)*

———

*Champagne*
*Lombardy Green Tart (page 32)*
*Crumb-Crusted Duckling Halves (page 64)*
*Cumberland Sauce (page 22)*
*French-Style Peas (page 67)   Whipped Carrots and Pears (page 68)*
*Burgundy or Pinot Noir Wine*
*Red Vegetable Salad (page 80)*
*Raspberry Mousse (see Fruit Mousse, page 87)*

## CASUAL SUPPERS

*Beet Mousse (page 77)*
*Chicken Meringue (page 62)*
*Peaches and Cream (page 84)*

———

*Yogurt Soup (page 35)*
*Lamb Ratatouille (page 44)*
*Mushrooms Stuffed with Garlic-Parsley Sauce (page 20)*
*Bordeaux or Cabernet Sauvignon Wine*
*Carrot-Apricot Tart (page 83)*

———

*Fresh Bean Sprout Salad (page 76)*
*Oriental One-Pot Meal (page 39)*
*Small Bowls of Rice*
*Hot Tea*
*Baked Banana and Orange Compote (page 85)*

———

*Savory Cheese Custards (page 33)*
*Meat-Stuffed Cabbage (page 41)*
*Whipped Carrots with Dill (page 68)*
*Crisp Gherkins*
*Red Wine*
*Fresh Fruit with Brandy Cream (page 84)*

## SMALL SIT-DOWN COMPANY DINNERS

*Spiced Pumpkin Soup (page 36)*
*Steak with Mushroom Stuffing (page 38)*
*Green Onions with Mock Hollandaise (page 70)*
*Red Bordeaux or Cabernet Sauvignon Wine*
*Fresh Spinach Salad (page 78)*
*Dessert Puff with Fruit (page 82)*

---

*Lombardy Green Tart (page 32)*
*Veal Scallops in Lemon Sauce (page 46)*
*Herbed Stuffed Mushrooms (page 67)*
*Light Red Wine, such as Beaujolais*
*Garden Vegetables in Sweet Seasoned Vinegar (page 79)*
*Peaches and Cream (page 84)*

---

*Cauliflower Soup (see Cauliflower Sauce, page 19)*
*Ducklings with Green Peppercorn Sauce (page 63)*
*Brussels Sprouts and Grapes (page 70)*
*Burgundy or Pinot Noir Wine*
*Red Vegetable Salad in Lettuce Cups (page 80)*
*Sliced Poached Pears in Wine with Custard Sauce (page 86)*

---

*Seviche in Lemon Cups (page 31)*
*Chicken with Poached Garlic (page 59)*
*French-Style Peas (page 67)   Gingered Turnips (page 71)*
*Chablis Wine*
*Vegetable Salad with Yogurt Dressing (page 79)*
*Cheese-Stuffed Strawberries (page 83)*

---

*Crab Meat Soup with Sherry (page 53)*
*Cornish Hens Normandy (page 58)*
*Composed Vegetable Platter (page 71) with Green Onion Sauce (page 23)*
*Vouvray or Chenin Blanc Wine*
*Oriental Cucumber Salad (page 79)*
*Molded Cheese Dessert (page 83)*

---

*Spinach Soup with Onion Petals (page 35)*
*Mock Crab Meat Salad with Melon Rings (page 56)*
*Capon with Vegetable Dressing (page 61)*
*Broiled Tomatoes with Piquant Sauce (page 69)*
*Moselle or Rhine Wine*
*Mocha Mousse (page 87)*

---

*White Vegetable Soup (see White Vegetable Purée, page 24)*
*Chilled Artichoke Plate (page 31)*
*Mock Hollandaise Sauce (page 22)*
*Crab-Stuffed Trout with Tarragon (page 52)*
*Broiled Tomatoes Parmesan*
*Moselle or Other Light White Wine*
*Pineapple-Berry Dessert (page 84)*

## FAMILY DINNERS

*Cucumbers with Buttermilk Dressing (page 78)*
*Pot Roast Jardinière (page 39)*
*Banana-Sweet Potato Bake (page 88)*
———
*Beet Mousse (page 77)*
*Hearty Beef-Cabbage Soup (page 41)*
*French Bread*
*Baked Sherried Bananas (page 85)*
———
*Egg-Drop Soup (page 34)*
*Pork Chops Piquant (page 44)*
*Cauliflower with Seasoned Dark Green Sauce (page 69)*
*Bibb Lettuce with Vinaigrette Dressing (page 24)*
*Hot Apple-Raisin Compote (page 86)*
———
*Celery Appetizer (page 32)*
*Stuffed Veal Breast (page 47)*
*Squash and Tomatoes Parmesan (page 69)*
*Fresh Fruit*
———
*Red Cabbage-Apple Salad (page 77)*
*Ham Steak with Parsley Sauce (page 45)*
*Baked Cheddar Onions (page 70)*
*Pineapple Sherbet*
———
*Roast Chicken Tarragon (page 59)*
*Mashed Carrots*
*Green Bean and Onion Salad (page 76)*
*Baked Banana and Orange Compote (page 85)*
———
*Sole Véronique in Parchment (page 53)*
*Boiled Potatoes with Cauliflower Sauce (page 19)*
*Green Beans*
*Peach Mousse (See Fruit Mousse, page 87)*

# INDEX